D1527489

*The Far Western Frontier*

*The Far Western Frontier*

*Advisory Editor*

## RAY A. BILLINGTON

Senior Research Associate
at the Henry E. Huntington Library
and Art Gallery

# HISTORY

### OF THE

# REVOLUTION IN TEXAS

#### PARTICULARLY OF THE

## WAR OF 1835 & '36

C[HESTER] NEWELL

## ARNO PRESS

**A NEW YORK TIMES COMPANY**
New York • 1973

DAVID GLENN HUNT
MEMORIAL LIBRARY
GALVESTON COLLEGE

Reprint Edition 1973 by Arno Press Inc.

Reprinted from a copy in The State
Historical Society of Wisconsin Library

The Far Western Frontier
ISBN for complete set: 0-405-04955-2
See last pages of this volume for titles.

Manufactured in the United States of America

———————————

**Library of Congress Cataloging in Publication Data**

Newell, Chester.
    History of the revolution in Texas, particularly of
the war of 1835 & '36.

    (The Far Western frontier)
    Reprint of the 1838 ed.
    1.  Texas--History--Revolution, 1835-1836.
2.  Texas--Description and travel.  I.  Title.
II.  Series.
F390.N54  1973        976.4'03        72-9462
ISBN 0-405-04990-0

# HISTORY

OF THE

# REVOLUTION IN TEXAS,

PARTICULARLY OF THE

## WAR OF 1835 & '36;

TOGETHER WITH THE

## LATEST GEOGRAPHICAL, TOPOGRAPHICAL, AND STATISTICAL

## ACCOUNTS OF THE COUNTRY,

*FROM THE MOST AUTHENTIC SOURCES.*

ALSO,

## AN APPENDIX.

## BY THE REV. C. NEWELL.

NEW-YORK

PUBLISHED BY WILEY & PUTNAM,
No. 161 Broadway.
( J. P. WRIGHT, PRINTER, CEDAR STREET. )

1 8 3 8 .

DAVID GLENN HUNT
MEMORIAL LIBRARY
GALVESTON COLLEGE

Entered according to an Act of Congress, in the year 1838, by
CHESTER NEWELL,
In the Clerk's Office of the District Court for the Southern District
of New-York.

TO THE HON. W. C. PRESTON,

*South Carolina :*

S I R,

Partaking of the chivalry which characterizes the People of the State which you ably represent in the councils of your country, reflecting honor on your constituents, and adding a lustre to the character of the American statesman, you have been among the first to raise your voice in behalf of the People of Texas, oppressed and calumniated. You have been actuated, as that people believe, by generous and noble sentiments; and of your support of their cause they are justly proud. As a small, though, I trust, not discreditable acknowledgment of that support, I avail myself of the privilege and the honor of DEDICATING to you the following work.

With sentiments of the highest consideration and respect,

Your obedient servant,

CHESTER NEWELL.

## TO THE READER.

THE following work is the result of a twelvemonth's residence in Texas, whither the Author repaired early in the Spring of 1837, for the benefit of his health. Three months of the twelve he spent at the capital of the Republic, exclusively and diligently employed in acquiring the information and material necessary for his work. He obtained valuable matter from docu. ments in the War Department, and others to which he had access; and also, much important information from repeated conversations with several men distinguished in the war of '35–'36,—of whom he will name His Excellency Gen. Houston, Gen. Lamar, Gen. F. Huston, Col. Poe, Col. Ward, Col. Neil, and Capt. Shackleford.

In the composition of his work, the Author has studied conciseness and perspicuity, more than elegance—to be useful, rather than original; and he submits to the Public the result of his labors, conscious that, in all he has written, he has endeavored to exhibit the *truth*.

0*

# CONTENTS.

---

## INTRODUCTION.

MEXICO—Brief Sketch of the History of Mexico from 1821 to 1835, . . . . . . . . . . . page 7

TEXAS—Effects of the Colonization of Texas by North Americans. Principal Object of the Writer. Objects of the Mexican Government in allowing the Colonization of Texas by North Americans. Conditions of that Colonization. Privileges, &c. of the Colonists. Progress of Colonization till 1827. Affair of Edwards at Nacogdoches, and its results. Oppressive Acts of the Mexican Government. . . . . 13

## CHAPTER I.

Mexican Garrisons in Texas. Peaceable Disposition of the Colonists. Oppressive Acts of the Military. The Results—Investment of the Fort at Anahuac—Capture of the Forts at Velasco and Nacogdoches—Arrival of Col. Mexia, and his Inquiries into late Disturbances. . . . . . . 23

## CHAPTER II.

Measures adopted for obtaining a State Government. Their Result in the Imprisonment of Gen. Austin in the Dungeons of the Inquisition in Mexico. Effect of the Intelligence of the same in Texas. . . . . . . . . 31

## CHAPTER III.

Difficulties at Monclova, and their results.  Sale of 44 leagues of Land, and its result, in the Dispersion, by the Troops of the General Government, of the Legislature at Monclova, and the effects of the same in Texas.  Peaceable Disposition of a Majority of the Colonists. . . . . . . page 37

## CHAPTER IV.

The Immediate Causes of the War which commenced in 1835. Affair of Thompson.  Appearance and Address of Gen. Austin.  Order of Gen. Cos for the Arrest of Zavala and others. Order from the same Officer, requiring the Citizens of certain Towns in Texas to deliver up their Arms.  Plan adopted by the Texans.  Circulars conveying Intelligence of the Approach of a Hostile Force under Gen. Cos, and making public a Letter from the Minister of Interior Relations in Mexico. Remarks upon the Letter.  Battle near Gonzales. . . 45

## CHAPTER V.

Prompt and Spirited Movements of the Texans.  Appointment of Samuel Houston as General of Department.  Opinions of Zavala.  Interest manifested in New Orleans in behalf of Texas.  Taking of Goliad.  General Council.  Meeting of the Consultation.  Address of Hon. B. T. Archer.  Election of Governor and Lieut. Governor.  Address of Gov. Smith.  55

## CHAPTER VI.

Siege and Capture of Bexar by the Texans. . . . . 67

## CHAPTER VII.

Gen. Houston appointed Commander-in-Chief.  Acts of the Provisional Government.  Decree of the General Congress of Mexico of the 3d of October.  Sympathy of the People of the

United States. Matamoras Expedition. Question of the Declaration of Independence. . . . . . page 72

## CHAPTER VIII.

Approach of Santa Anna and his Army. Siege and Capture of the Alamo by the Mexicans. . . . . . . 81

## CHAPTER IX.

Meeting of the Convention at Washington. Head-Quarters of the Army at Gonzales. Fate of the two Detachments sent out from Goliad, under King and Ward. Evacuation of Goliad by Fannin. Battle near Goliad. Surrender and Massacre of Fannin and his men. . . . . . . 92

## CHAPTER X.

Formation of a Government *ad interim*. Retreat of Gen. Houston to the Colorado. Advance of the Mexicans. Retreat of Houston to the Brazos. Advance of Santa Anna. Battle of San Jacinto. . . . . . . . 101

## CHAPTER XI.

Treaties with Santa Anna. Protests of Santa Anna. Answer to the same by President Burnet. . . . . . 109

## CHAPTER XII.

Evacuation of Texas by the Mexican Army under Filisola. Volunteers from the United States—Interest there excited in behalf of Texas. Excitement in Mexico, caused by the Reverses of Santa Anna. Question on the Disposal of Santa Anna. . . . . . . . . . 115

## CHAPTER XIII.

Constitutional Election of President, Vice-President, and Members of Congress. Acts of the First Congress. . . . 120

## GEOGRAPHY, &c. OF TEXAS.

General Features, . . . . . . . . page 129

Larger Divisions. . . . . . . . . . 130

Principal Rivers, and Adjacent Country. . . . . 132

Secondary Rivers. . . . . . . . . 137

Principal Towns, and Adjacent Country. . . . . 139

Minor Towns. . . . . . . . . . . 149

Sea-board Towns—Commercial Advantages, Bays, Harbors, &c. 157

Prospective Trade of Texas. . . . . . . . 164

Products—Cotton, Sugar, Grapes, Silk, &c. . . . . 165

Minerals. . . . . . . . . . . 171

Mineral Springs. . . . . . . . . . 173

Timber. . . . . . . . . . . 174

Prairies. . . . . . . . . . . 176

River Scenery. . . . . . . . . . 178

To the Merchant. . . . . . . . . . 179

To Mechanics. . . . . . . . . . 181

To the Emigrant. . . . . . . . . . 181

Education. . . . . . . . . . . 185

Morals. . . . . . . . . . . 186

Religion. . . . . . . . . . . 189

APPENDIX. . . . . . . . . . 192–215

# HISTORY

### OF THE

# REVOLUTION IN TEXAS.

# INTRODUCTION.

## MEXICO.

ABOUT the time of the establishment of the first American Colonists in Texas, Mexico had achieved her Independence of Old Spain. In 1821, Don Augustin Iturbide, a Royal officer, availing himself of half a million of dollars, with which he had been entrusted, and assisted by Guerrero and Victoria, revolted from the Spanish Government. The result was, in 1822, the assembling of a National Congress, and the establishment of a limited monarchy, in conformity with the plan of Iquala and the Treaty of Cordova. The Spanish Constitution was also provisionally adopted. The Executive Department was administered by a Regency, of which Iturbide was chosen President, who was also appointed Admiral and Generalissimo of the Army and Navy, with a salary of $12,000.

Serious dissensions soon arose between the Generalissimo and Congress, and the Regency were divided.

One of its principal and most liberal members had a personal dispute, of great warmth, with Iturbide, during one of the sittings, in which the terms *traitor* and *usurper* were mutually passed. The friends of Liberty were alarmed at the ascendency which the Generalissimo had acquired over the military and the populace. On the night of the 18th of May, the soldiery and populace, headed by sergeants and corporals, proclaimed Iturbide Emperor. It was a night of violence, confusion, and uproar. The seven hundred bells of the capital pealed from the steeples of monasteries, convents, and churches; cannon and musketry were fired from the barracks; and the shouts of the populace proclaimed that a few soldiers and a city mob had taken it upon them to decide the fate of Mexico. The session of Congress on the 19th was held surrounded by bayonets, and the man who was thus proclaimed by a rabble, in darkness and tumult, was, by a decree of the Congress, declared to be Emperor of Mexico.

On the 31st of October following, the Congress was turned out of doors by an armed force, acting in obedience to a decree of the Emperor, which declared Congress to be dissolved, and which vested the legislative power of the nation in a Junta Instituyente, the members of which were nominated by himself.

On the 2d of December, Gen. Santa Anna, who commanded at Vera Cruz, raised the standard of opposition to the arbitrary proceedings of Iturbide; and on the

6th, in union with the civil authorities of Vera Cruz,
published a "plan," the basis of which was the re-union
of the Congress, which had been dispersed by the order
of the Emperor, and a guarantee that its deliberations
should be free from military restraint.    Gen. Victoria,
who had been imprisoned in November, 1821, by Iturbide, and had escaped in February, 1822, suddenly appeared from his retreat, and joined the Congress and
Santa Anna party.  A severe, though not decisive, battle was fought at Xalapa, between Santa Anna and the
Imperial troops.   About the same time, Generals Guerrero and Bravo also took the field in favor of the Congress.  On the 2d day of February, the army, which was
besieging Santa Anna at Vera Cruz, revolted from the
Emperor, joined the besieged, declared for Congress,
and published another "plan" similar to that of Santa
Anna's, called the plan of Casa Mata.    These events
gave impulse to the Revolution, which spread through
the provinces of Puebla, Oaxaca, and parts of Mexico.
Other States, however, appeared to remain quiet;
though, since the defection of Santa Anna, a general
suspense and anxiety had prevailed, which was daily
becoming more intense.    On the 20th and 21st of February, information was circulated in the capital of a
general defection of those parts of the nation which had
till then remained passive, and Iturbide began to be pub-
licly spoken of as an usurper.  Early in February he had

1*

marched out of the city at the head of all the troops he could collect, and occupied a station at Istapaluca. But, finding that he could not rely upon his troops, and that the force marching against him from Puebla greatly exceeded his own, and was daily augmenting, he consented to a cessation of hostilities, and Commissioners were appointed to treat. The Commissioners met, and agreed, in substance, that the Emperor should retire to Tacubaya; that Congress should be convened as soon as practicable, and that all parties should submit to whatever it might dictate; that neither party should have troops in the capital; and that the necessary guards to keep order should be at the disposal of the civil authorities until the meeting of Congress. That body convened on the 29th of March, and decided that the Sovereign Constituent Congress of Mexico was in legal session, and that its deliberations were free from restraint; that the Executive power, which had existed since the 19th of May, 1822, had ceased. On the 31st, Congress decreed that the Executive power of the nation should be provisionally deposited in a body to be styled the *Supreme Executive Power*, to be composed of three individuals. On the same day Nicholas Bravo, Guadalupe Victoria, and Pedro Celestino Negrette, were chosen the Executive Power. A re-organization of the Government took place. On the 8th of April, Congress decreed that the coronation of Iturbide was an act of violence and force, and was null;

and that hereditary succession, and all titles emanating from the Emperor, were null; and that all the acts of the last Government were illegal; and that, finally, Iturbide was forever banished from the Mexican territory, but that he should receive annually $25,000, (provided he resided in Italy,) and that after his death his family should have an annual pension of $8000.

On the 17th of June, 1823, Congress decreed that a new Constituent Congress should be elected by the people, for the express purpose of adopting the form of government, forming the Constitution, and organizing the nation, agreeably to the will of the people.

On the 19th of the same month, Congress passed a resolution directing the Supreme Executive Power to inform the people that the existing Congress were in favor of a Federal Republican system of Government.

The first Congress closed its sessions on the 30th of October, and the second, elected in virtue of the decree of the 17th of June, opened its sessions on the 5th of November. On the 31st of January, 1824, Congress decreed the Act of Confederation, by which the Federal system was formally adopted as the basis of the Government.

In the course of the year 1824 several insurrections broke out; one of which, headed by Echavani and Hernandez, was quelled by Guerrero; another, headed by Lobato, the object of which was to compel Congress to dismiss European Spaniards from office, was also quelled, and the cause removed. In the month of July Iturbide again made his appearance. By a decree of Congress of the 28th of April he had been declared a traitor, and out of the protection of the law, if he should again set foot within the Mexican territory. He was taken at Paraje de los Arroyos, sent to Padilla, and, by the order of the State Congress convened at that place, was shot on the 19th of July.

On the 15th, Guadalupe Victoria, President of the Republic, issued a decree, abolishing forever all traffic in slaves.

In 1825, titles of nobility were abolished, and the power of the priests much diminished. The last vestige of the power of Old Spain was obliterated in Mexico by the surrender of the garrison at Vera Cruz to the ship Asia. The Independence of Mexico was acknowledged by Great Britain.

In 1826, the question of the suppressing Masonic Lodges, in obedience to a bull of the Pope, caused much excitement. A bill for the purpose was introduced into Congress, but rejected. Most of the influential men in Mexico sided with one or the other of two factions, said to be under the guidance of the rival Scotch and York Lodges. The Escoces, or Scotch faction, were large proprietors, moderate, and favorable to the establishment of a Royal Government. The Yorkinos were opposed to a Royal Government.

In 1827, a storm burst forth at Olumba, where Don

Jose Montano published his plan of a forcible reform of the Government, in opposition to the Yorkinos.

In 1828, Gen. Bravo, Vice-President of the Republic, declared for the rebels, and stationed himself at Tulancingo, where he issued a manifesto in favor of Montano. Gen. Vincente Guerrero took the field in favor of the Government, and the result was, that Bravo and his associates were banished the Republic. The two parties were again arrayed against each other at the election of a President in September, to succeed Victoria. After an arduous contest, the Escoces candidate, Manuel Gomez Pedraza, was chosen by a majority of two votes over Guerrero, the candidate of the Yorkinos. Santa Anna, at the head of a body of troops, declared this vote not an expression of the popular will, and proclaimed Guerrero President. Not at first successful, he again took the field, assisted by Lobato and Zavala. Finally, Guerrero himself appeared in arms. In December, civil war raged in all its horrors in Mexico. The result, after much bloodshed, was the flight of Pedraza, who gave up his claims to the Presidency and left the country.

Guerrero was elected to succeed Pedraza on the 6th of January, 1829. Anastasio Bustamente was chosen Vice-President, and Santa Anna Secretary of War.

On the 27th of July, an expedition of four thousand men, fitted out at Havana to subjugate Mexico, landed at Tampico. After a contest of two months, this force

surrendered to Santa Anna on the 10th day of September.

Intestine collisions were soon renewed. Guerrero
was unwilling to lay aside the authority of Dictator,
with which he had been invested : hence another Revolution.   Bustamente placed himself at the head of a
body of troops in December, and issued a proclamation,
denouncing Executive abuses.   Guerrero was forced
to abdicate, and Bustamente was immediately elected
in his place.   In the latter part of the year 1829 new
troubles arose : Guerrero, the late President, established
a form of government at Valladolid in opposition to
Bustamente, and soon the whole country was in arms
again.

In February, 1831, Guerrero, who had retired to his
native section of the country, near Acapulco, was there
treacherously made prisoner by one Picaluga, a Sar-
dinian or Italian, delivered up to the military authorities of a small port in the State of Oaxaca, and there
tried and shot by order of Government.

In 1832, the troops of Gen. Teran were cut to pieces
by those of Montezuma.

In 1834, Santa Anna, who had been of the Republican
party, joined that of the church and the aristocrats,
and set himself in opposition to the cause he had hitherto sustained.   On the 13th of May he dissolved the
Mexican Congress before its term had expired, issued
an order for the assembling of another, and dissolved

the Council of Government, which he took into his own hands.

On the 1st of January, 1835, a new Congress met. Contrary pronunciamentos, petitions, and protests, were sent in by the military and the people. Those of the latter were disregarded, and their authors persecuted; those of the former received as the voice of the nation. The Vice-President, Gomez Ferias, was deposed, and Gen. Barragan elected in his place. In April, Alvarez, Governor of Zacatecas, revolted against the acts of the Congress, which, under Santa Annà and the church, was issuing decrees subversive of the Republic, and preparing the way for a despotic Government. In May, the hopes of the Federal party were nearly extinguished by a victory gained by Santa Anna over Alvarez. Gutirez and Victoria took the field against the victor, but the latter was invariably successful. In June the plan of Toluca was adopted and published, by which the Government became Central and consolidated.

# TEXAS.

AUSPICIOUS to the interests of humanity—to the extension of liberty, of knowledge, and of liberal principles, was the establishment of a Colony in Texas by Stephen F. Austin, in 1821–2. It was establishing the Anglo-American race one remove farther to the South and West, in the then all but impassable barrier between the civilized and free States of the North and the remains of despotism and barbarism of the South—in a land then a wilderness, and the home of the savage, but now redeemed and free—a land of the orange, the fig, and the vine; the Italy of America, where delightful breezes " blow soft," where " every prospect pleases," and where Nature has bestowed her riches and her beauties with a lavish hand—a land towards which, as towards the Italy of the old world, the hardy people of the North are pouring in a ceaseless tide of emigration, and where is destined to be a great, wealthy, and powerful nation.

This country was, from the first, inviting, as well for

2

the great fertility of its soil, as the salubrity of its climate and the beauty of its scenery.  Americans emigrated to it to improve their condition, to get lands,
and eventually to amass wealth.  They reclaimed it
from a wilderness and from the savage, and then
took the government of it into their own hands.
For this last act, they have been charged with mercenary views, and with ingratitude ; and opprobrium
without measure has been heaped upon them.  Their
motives and their acts have not been sufficiently known
nor understood.  It is the principal object of the writer, in the following work, faithfully and impartially to
exhibit the causes and narrate the interesting events of
the Revolution, which has placed Texas in the attitude
of an Independent Nation.  That the reader may have
a better understanding of those causes and events, a
brief exposition will first be given of the objects the
Mexican Government had in view in allowing the
Colonization of Texas by North Americans, of the conditions on which it was allowed, and also of the rights,
privileges, and encouragement of the Colonists.

The leading object of the Mexican Government in
allowing the Colonization of Texas, was undoubtedly
the protection of her frontiers from the hostile incur-
sions of the Indians.  The Camanches and other tribes
had waged a constant and ruinous warfare against the
Spanish settlements at Bexar and Goliad, on the Western limits of Texas, and had extended their ravages

also beyond the Rio Grande.   Mexico, even under the government of Old Spain, had been unable to subdue or restrain them, and she would have had to abandon Texas altogether, if not other parts of her territory, had she not found a hardy people, willing, for the sake of a small portion of her soil, to go in and subdue them.

Another object which Mexico had in view, in opening Texas to Colonization, was evidently the increase of her national wealth and strength by the settlement of a rich portion of her territory by industrious and enterprising foreigners, which she knew could never be subdued and settled by her own people.

In addition to this, Mexico was probably stimulated somewhat by the example of the liberal and successful plan adopted by the United States of the North, in respect to the emigration of foreigners into her territory, as she had previously been, by the successful revolution of those States, excited to throw off the Spanish yoke.

The conditions of the grant of the Colonization of Texas were, on the part of Mexico, that the families introduced should be limited in number—at first to 300 ; that they should be families from Louisiana, and Catholics, being hence of Spanish and French descent ; that they should build churches, support schools and the Catholic religion, and particularly have their children taught the Spanish language.   These conditions are especially worthy of notice, as affording evidence that the Government of Mexico contemplated the ultimate amalgamation of her foreign emigrants with her own people, and thus securing the integrity of her territory and dominion.

The rights of the Colonists consisted in security of person and property, guaranteed to them by the Imperial Colonization Law of 1823, by the Federal Law and Constitution of 1824, and also, subsequently, by the laws and Constitution of the State of Coahuila and Texas.

An important part of the property of the Colonists consisted in the slaves which they were permitted to introduce into Texas previous to the year 1827. By the Imperial Colonization Law of 1823, all traffic in slaves was prohibited; and by the same law it was made necessary for the Colonists to liberate their slaves born in Texas at fourteen years of age; but the introduction of slaves into Texas was not prohibited until 1827.

By the law of 1823, the Colonists were privileged to introduce, at the time of their emigration to the country, instruments of husbandry, machinery, and other utensils, free, as also merchandise—in case of the emigration of a family—to the amount of two thousand dollars.

By the Federal Law of 1824, it was provided, that, until the expiration of four years after the passage of the law, no tax whatever should be imposed upon foreigners emigrating to Texas. By subsequent laws, especially of Coahuila and Texas, this privilege of foreign emigrants was confirmed and extended.

The great encouragement to foreigners to emigrate to Texas, was the liberal bounty of land proffered them by the Government of Mexico. Land was given in quantities varying with the occupation and the wants of emigrants, on a scale of liberality undoubtedly not equalled in the Colonization of any other country.

Besides this, the Government guaranteed to foreigners a continuation of the privilege of emigrating to Texas until the year 1840, unless "imperious circumstances" should require its prohibition "with respect to the individuals of a particular nation."

To complete the introduction to our work, it will be necessary to acquaint the reader with a few of the most important events in the history of Texas down to the year 1832, when we shall consider the revolutionary ball as having began to roll.

For several years the work of Colonization went on well, interrupted only by occasional difficulties with Indians. There was a good understanding between the Colonists and the General and State Governments. General Austin was highly esteemed wherever known in Mexico, and able to obtain almost any redress or privilege in the power of Government to bestow. All who applied obtained lands equal to their most sanguine expectations. They were exempt from taxes and imposts of every kind, and were relieved of all the

2*

onerous duties imposed upon the rest of the people of
Mexico.   This state of things continued down to the
affair of Edwards at Nacogdoches in 1827.   This excited a good deal of attention, and has been more generally known and spoken of, because supposed by many
to have been an extensive plot for the subjugation of
all Mexico, with which, it has been asserted, the celebrated Aaron Burr was leagued.   The history of this,
so far as known, is as follows :   Edwards, as Empresario, had obtained from the Mexican Government the
right of colonizing a portion of country around and
including Nacogdoches.   Either not understanding, or
disposed to pervert to his own interests the laws under
which he obtained his right or grant, he represented
to his Colonists that he held the lands within the limits
of that grant in fee simple, and had a right to sell the
same, and accordingly charged the Colonists a certain
sum per acre for their land.   This they soon found to
be an imposition, and resolved not to submit to it.
They petitioned the Government for redress, whereupon
the grant to Edwards was revoked.   Thinking this
act of the Government oppressive, Edwards raised the
standard of revolt, and invited the neighboring Indians
to join him.   The Government, upon information of
this, sent a force to put him down.   The Colonists of
Western Texas, opposed to the movement of Edwards,
joined this force, whereupon Edwards, finding himself
unsustained, abandoned the country.

In this difficulty, the Colonists were by no means im-
plicated, and yet it had a very perceptible effect in
diminishing the confidence of the Government of Mexico in their loyalty. Troops began to be introduced
into Texas, but cautiously, in small numbers at different times, to prevent alarm. Companies of from twelve
to twenty men were sent into the country, some ostensibly to convey despatches, some specie, and some for
other purposes. These men did not return, but were
garrisoned at Nacogdoches, until, from sixty or seventy
men, the number there amounted to two hundred and
fifty. Soon the Government established other garrisons
in Texas, ostensibly to secure its revenue, and to protect the Colonists from Indian depredations, but really,
as a leading object—as the Colonists well knew—to secure its power in Texas. Yet they neither resisted nor
complained, until the power of the Government, thus
established, began to exhibit itself in acts of oppression. Of these, the first was the decree of 1829, pro-
mulgated by Guerrero, then President of the Republic,
declaring all slaves throughout Mexico to be free.
This decree, as the reader will readily perceive, was in
violation of the vested constitutional rights of the Colonists, and was evidently an act of high-handed oppression ; for even had the laws been violated on the
part of the Colonists, by the introduction of slaves into
Texas, the proper redress would have been for the
Government to have put those laws into execution.

The Colonists complained, and after considerable nego-
ciation, by means of Viesca, then Governor of Coahuila
and Texas,—who represented the disastrous effects to
the Colonists of the liberation of their slaves,—obtained
from Guerrero the revocation of his decree as regarded
Texas.

The next oppressive act of the Government was the
passage of the notorious, and, more than all, odious law
of the 6th of April, 1830, prohibiting the farther emigration of North Americans to Texas, except in so
far as regarded the fulfilment of existing contracts.
Though, in the passage of this law, the Government
might be said to have availed itself only of its reserved
right of prohibiting the emigration of "individuals of
a particular nation," yet it was striking a death-blow
at the interests of the Colonies, and therefore oppressive.    Texas had been settled by North Americans;
North Americans had redeemed it from a wilderness
to the purposes of agriculture; and had made it, in place
of a solitary region, inhabited by the savage and the
wild beast, a country prosperous in a high degree,
having on its whole face inscribed the assurance of its
future greatness. They had been *invited* to Texas; had
expatriated themselves; given up the conveniences
and luxuries of life; and, for years, had encountered
toils, dangers, and privations of every sort.    They had
given security to the Mexican frontiers from Indian
depredations, and made the mountains the boundary

of the savage. And, having accomplished all this, the Government was about to deprive them of that for which they had labored and suffered : the inevitable conse-quence of forbidding the farther emigration of their countrymen to Texas.

This law was suspended in its operation, but never revoked. That it was enacted from mere caprice, without any cause, it would be doing the Government of Mexico injustice to suppose. Its Colonization Laws were doubtless, to some extent, evaded and violated by North Americans, but this was mostly, if not entirely, on the part of non-residents in Texas. If, therefore, the Government had been disposed to act justly, and pro-tect, instead of oppressing, its subjects, it would have enforced its laws against those who had violated them.

# HISTORY

# REVOLUTION IN TEXAS.

———

## CHAPTER I.

In 1832—a year memorable in Texas, for being that in which the Colonies first took up arms in defence of their rights—the General Government of Mexico had garrisoned soldiers in Texas, nearly as follows: at Nacogdoches, 500 ; at Bexar, 250 ; at Goliad, 118 ; at Anahuac, 150 ; at Galveston, 30 ; at Velasco, 100 ; at Ft. Teran, 40 ; at Victoria, 40 ; at Tenoxticlan, 40.

To one acquainted, on the one hand, with the generally licentious character of the soldiers of a standing army, and particularly that of the soldiers of Mexico, where the military are permitted to rule and the people to submit,—and, on the other, with the character of North Americans, obedient to law, and universally jealous of their rights,—it must be perfectly evident that Mexican soldiers and North American citizens could not live together without collision. And yet the Colonists were generally desirous of peace. Tired and disgusted, many of them, with the noise and rancor of

party strife in the United States, they had emigrated to
Texas in search of peace and quiet, as well as a more
genial soil and a milder clime.  The peaceful dense
groves, which they there found,—the extended verdant
prairies, where the primitive repose of Nature was only
here and there disturbed by the settler's axe, or by the
lowing of his cattle on the prairie,—more than satisfied
them—they were delighted with the land of their
adoption ; and, grateful for the liberal boon which had
been bestowed upon them by the Mexican Government,
they were anxious to preserve the harmony which had
hitherto, for the most part, existed between themselves
and that Government.   But peace was not now at the
option of the Colonists, unless by an entire surrender of
rights which in childhood they had been taught, and in
manhood believed, to be sacred ; which they esteemed
of vital importance to their welfare, as a people, and
which, having always enjoyed, they valued as highly as
life itself.   Such rights they could not surrender, and
such were now trampled upon by the authorities, especially the military, of Mexico ; and the constitution
and laws of the country seemed to be entirely disregarded.   This state of things, which had now become
intolerable, had been in progress for more than a year.
The first overt act of the military in Texas was the
arrest and imprisonment, in 1831, of a Commissioner,
appointed by the Government of the State of Coahuila
and Texas to put certain emigrants in possession of
lands which had been previously opened to Colonization
by the General Government.   The imprisonment of
this Commissioner was by the order of the Commandant General of the Eastern Province of Mexico, because

in alleged contravention of the law of the 6th of April, 1830. Even if it were in contravention of that law, as it was not allowed to be by the Governor of Coahuila and Texas, the imprisonment by the military of a civil officer, whilst in the peaceable discharge of the duties of his office, and without trial, was evidently unconstitutional and oppressive, and done in disregard, if not contempt, of both law and right.

The next unconstitutional act of the military in Texas, was the annulling of one Ayuntamiento, legally established by the authority of the Government of the State of Coahuila and Texas, and the substitution of another without authority from that Government and without consulting it ; and subsequently, when, by the authority of the same Government, there was about to be an election of officers of the Ayuntamiento so annulled, a military commandant issued orders forbidding the election, and threatening military force if it were proceeded with.

The next and last oppressive act of the military, during the period now under consideration, which struck at the root of Liberty in the Colonies, was the arrest and imprisonment of several Anglo-American Colonists. To this it was impossible that Americans should submit. They did not submit ; but, in that manly, firm, and determined manner which has characterised their ancestors in their great struggle for liberty, without noise and confusion, and almost without preconcert, they armed, assembled, and appeared before the garrison in which their fellow-citizens had been imprisoned, and there demanded redress, which, if refused, they were about to take into their own hands.

3

The commandant, not daring to resist, promised to release his prisoners; requesting a little time to be allowed him first, to make out or arrange some necessary
documents. This the Colonists granted, and trusting
to his word and honor, were leaving the garrison,
when he, in a treacherous manner, characteristic of his
nation, opened a fire upon them, aware no doubt of the
near approach of reinforcements by which he expected
to be sustained. The Colonists turned to attack him,
when they unexpectedly fell in with a force under
Piedras, commandant of the garrison at Nacogdoches.
This was the expected reinforcement. Piedras found
himself cut off from the garrison he was approaching,
and being nearly surrounded, was obliged to surrender.
He was promised permission to return with his force
to Nacogdoches, on condition of his ordering the release
of the prisoners at Anahuac. This, (being the superior
of the officer there in command,) he did, and returned to
Nacogdoches. The Colonists, having attained their object, returned to their homes. Such is the wonderful
forbearance of intelligent freemen, contending for their
rights!

Whilst yet they were under arms, however, having
heard that the citizens of Vera Cruz, headed by Santa
Anna, had declared for the Constitution and Laws,
against the arbitrary administration of Bustamente, then
President of the Republic, they passed resolutions unanimously declaring their purpose to espouse the cause
of their fellow-citizens at Vera Cruz.

In the mean time, the citizens of the department of
the Brazos having intelligence both of the difficulties at
Anahuac and of the rise of the citizens of Vera Cruz,

resolved to espouse the cause of the latter, and to assist their fellow-citizens of the former place in obtaining redress of their grievances. But, first, they invited Ugartechea, commandant of the fort at Velasco, to join them in the support of the Liberal cause they had es-poused, and at the same time informed him, in a candid manner, of their purpose to march against Anahuac ; and counting upon his good offices for many kindnesses they had shown him, and for the good understanding which had existed between them, they requested him to permit them to take past the fort at Velasco, a cannon, with which they were desirous to proceed round by water to Anahuac ; and, furthermore, even requested him to protect their families and property in their ab-sence. Ugartechea refused to join them, and told them in a frank and gentleman-like manner, that the com-mandant at Anahuac being his superior, he was obliged to obey orders received from that officer ; that he could afford them no countenance ; and that, if they attempted to take a cannon past Velasco, he was bound to give them the best fight he could. " Well," said they, " we must then dislodge you first." Accordingly, they im-mediately assembled, to the number of 117, and attack-ed the fort on the morning of the 26th of June, before day. A battle ensued, next to that of the Alamo in '36, the bloodiest during the War of Independence in Texas. The Texans were gallantly led to the charge by their commander, John Austin ; but, whilst it was yet dark, directed in their fire only by the flash of their enemies' guns, and, exposed to the full effect, not only of the Mex-ican small arms, but of a cannon placed on a pivot upon a bastion of the fort, they suffered much ; whilst they

did little injury to the enemy, protected by the walls of
the fort.  With the return of day, however, the Texan
rifles had their wonted effect: every Mexican who showed his head above the walls of the fort was shot down ;
those  who  manned  the  cannon  were  repeatedly  shot
away ; till, at length, Ugartechea, having in vain endeavored to force his men to ascend the bastion, heroically
set  the  example  himself,  and  directed  the  gun.    Upon
this  the  Texans,  though  they  might  have  shot  an  eye
out  of  his  head,  respecting  Ugartechea  as  a  man,  and
admiring  his  courage  as  a  soldier,  generously  ceased
their  fire.    Ugartechea  surrendered.    Terms of capitulation  were  drawn  up  and  signed,  and  the  Mexicans,
both  officers  and  soldiers,  received  and  treated  as
friends.    In this battle there were of the Texans eleven
killed and fifty-two wounded—twelve of them mortally ;
of the Mexicans, one hundred and twenty-five of whom
were  in  the  garrison,  seventeen  had  their  hands  shot
off,  and  one  half  were  killed.    The  Colonists,  now
hearing  of  the  submission  of  the  commandant of Anahuac, returned to their homes.

   Thus had oppression been stifled in its strong-holds
by  the  sturdy  arm  of  freemen,  which  never  strikes  in
vain.    But yet the acts of the Texans, in accomplishing
this work, were doubtless of a rebellious character.  So
they  were  soon  represented  in  Mexico ;  and  Santa
Anna,  not  knowing  that  the  Texans  had  espoused  the
cause  of  the  Liberals  of  Mexico,  in  support  of  which
himself  and  the  Mexicans  under  his  command  had
taken  up  arms,  but  believing  their  object  to  be  the  separation of Texas from Mexico, despatched Col. Mexia
with  a force to put them down.    Mexia sailed from the

Brazos Santiago on the 14th of July, with five vessels and 400 men. Gen. Austin, the representative of Texas in the State Legislature, also embarked with Mexia, a circumstance very favorable to an early and good understanding between Mexia and the Colonists of Texas. On the 16th, the fleet anchored off the mouth of the Brazos. Mexia immediately addressed an official letter to the alcalde, John Austin, acquainting him with the object of his visit; and received in reply a detailed account of the late events in Texas, with a statement of the causes which led to them, and of the motives of the Texans in taking up arms. On the 17th, Mexia arrived at Brazoria, where he was treated with great respect and hospitality. He there received, at his particular request, a farther official and more particular account of the late events in Texas, drawn up at a meeting of citizens assembled for the purpose. In addition to this, at the request of an alcalde of Austin's Colony, there was convened at San Felippe a general representation of the different Ayuntamientos, for the purpose of investigating fully the causes of the late disturbances, and of ascertaining entirely the desires and views of the people of Texas, that a statement of the same might be presented to Mexia, and through him to Gen. Santa Anna. Such a statement† the representatives drew up and delivered to Mexia, accompanied with resolutions expressing their regret that the enemies of Texas should have represented them as entertaining views opposed to the integrity of the Mexican Republic; and that they had not been able, after every endeavor, to prevent the late

† See Appendix, No. 2.

3*

disturbances, owing to the arbitrary measures of Col. Bradburn; averring also their sincere desire, that the Government should be restored to its constitutional basis, and that they had no other object in view than to aid in sustaining the constitution and laws, which had been violated by the military. Mexia, satisfied with the representations of the Texans, soon departed with his fleet, taking with him the soldiers of the dismantled fort at Velasco, and such others as were disposed to join the Liberating Army in Mexico.

Soon after this, the citizens of Nacogdoches, who had heard of what had transpired at Anahuac and on the Brazos—and also that Piedras, commandant of the garrison at Nacogdoches, had been invited by Mexia to join the Liberating Army in Mexico, and had refused—took up arms, attacked Piedras, and compelled him to surrender, after an engagement of several hours, in which three Texans were killed and seven wounded; eighteen Mexicans killed, and twenty-two wounded.

Thus had the Texans thrown off the oppressive yoke of the military; and this they had done—owing to a fortunate movement in Mexico, simultaneously with their own, in favor of the constitution and laws—without the disastrous effects of a collision with the General Government.

## CHAPTER II.

Of the events which transpired between the summer of 1832, when the Texans laid down their arms, and their resort to them again in the summer of 1835, we propose to give only such an outline as will enable the reader to understand the causes which led to the latter event, and rightly to appreciate the motives of such as were active in bringing it about.

The people of Texas had now learned that the constitution and laws of the General Government were very much a dead letter; and they believed, that, though they had rid themselves of a galling military yoke, there was no security that the same would not be fastened on them again. Besides, there were existing many and great evils, for which a remedy was very much needed. There was an almost total want of a local government of any kind. The people were exceedingly ignorant of the laws by which they were governed,—of those even affecting their personal liberty and their lives. These laws were in an unknown language, and scattered through hundreds of volumes in distant portions of the Republic; the officers and courts of appeal, from the local authorities, were six hundred miles distant, at Monclova; months, and even years, might, and in some instances did, expire before even a hearing could be obtained. For these and other evils they were bound to provide a remedy; and, as freemen, they were bound, too, to provide some *security* for the main-

tenance of their own and their children's rights. This
was a great work before them, and attended with
greater difficulties, owing to the existing jealousy of the
Mexican Government; and when they now set about
it, it was not separation from that Government which
they sought, but to be constituted rather one of its
sovereign unities, having the management of their local
affairs in their own hands. They had been completely
trammelled in their connection with Coahuila; the necessity of a separation had been long felt, and had been
considerably agitated in 1830.- Moreover, Texas having
by a law of the 7th of May, 1824, been united to Coahuila *conditionally* only, until she should possess the
requisite elements to form a State by herself, and
having now those elements, had a right to claim a
separation from Coahuila, and to be admitted as a State
of the Mexican confederacy.

The first step the Texans therefore took, was to provide for the assembling of a convention of the People.
This convention assembled at San Felippe, where it held
its sessions during the latter part of the year 1832 and
the beginning of 1833. At this convention was drawn
up a constitution for the "State of Texas," which is
alike creditable to the understanding and loyalty of its
authors; a petition also to the General Government,*
which fully and ably represented the evils of a connection with Coahuila, and the reasons why Texas should
become a State by itself. The Constitution, as it forms
no part of the history of the times, except in the fact
of its being drawn up and forwarded to the General
Government, it is not necessary farther to notice; nor

* See Appendix, No. 3.

the petition, except in so far as it exhibits difficulties and grievances not already noticed. The petitioners respectfully represented that Coahuila and Texas were dissimilar in soil, climate, and productions—in common interests—and partly in population; that the representatives of the former were numerous, and those of the latter few—in consequence, any law passed especially to the benefit of Texas, was the effect only of a generous courtesy; that laws well adapted to promote the interests of Coahuila might be ruinous to Texas; that protection from Indian depredations was of vital importance to Texas, and that a wide intervening wilderness was an insuperable barrier in the way of her receiving efficient aid from Coahuila; that the Indians in their neighborhood, owing to the tardy, partial measures of the Government, and the dishonesty of her agents, had not been fairly dealt with; and that, as a State, Texas would be able to take prompt and efficient measures in their behalf.

Though the people of Texas had doubtless good and sufficient reasons for desiring a separation of Texas from Coahuila, yet the policy of petitioning the General Government for the accomplishment of that object, at the time of the existence in Mexico of great jealousy and distrust of the people of Texas, was, in the opinion of Gen. Austin, more than questionable; for he represents, that an excitement had been got up in favor of a State Government by "political fanatics," and those in favor of "high-handed measures with the Government," and that himself had been placed in the "alternative of yielding,—of opposing by means of party divisions,—or of leaving the country."

However opposed to the rash and high-handed measures of some in getting up a petition, which, at the
*time*, he thought inexpedient, yet, obedient to the popular will, when constitutionally and legally expressed,
Gen. Austin, the man of the people's choice, in April,
1833, set out for the city of Mexico, as commissioner,
to obtain from the General Government a redress of
various grievances, and particularly the separation of
Texas from Coahuila, and its recognition and reception as a State of the Confederacy.

Arrived in the metropolis of the nation, Gen. Austin
engaged heartily in the discharge of the duties of his
mission, as well from a conviction of the necessity to
Texas of a State Government, as a regard to the duty he
owed his constituents. He urged the claims of Texas in
a pressing manner, representing that its affairs required
the prompt attention of Government, and that " the people there had taken the position, that if the evils which
threatened the ruin of the country were not remedied,
the people of Texas would remedy them of themselves."
This, so plain and candid representation, was construed
into a threat, though none was intended ; and Austin,
after having for months labored in vain to obtain for the
people of Texas either a State Government or the redress of their grievances, in the month of October
wrote home, advising the people to form a State *de
facto* of themselves. As grounds for this advice, many
circumstances doubtless came under the observation of
Austin, of which he alone could rightly judge. To one
at a distance, and unacquainted with those circumstances, the advice may seem to savor of rashness ;
and yet it is known to all, that the Government of

Mexico was in a very uncertain, weak, and disorganized state, and that the period seemed remote when
it should be in more healthy and vigorous action.
However, the letter of Austin proved a misfortune to himself, if not to Texas. Addressed to the Ayuntamiento of
Bexar, it was there opened and immediately sent back to
Mexico. Austin, who in the mean time had departed
from the capital, was pursued and overtaken at Saltillo, six hundred miles distant, conducted back to
Mexico as a prisoner, and cast as a criminal into a
dungeon of the Inquisition, where he was kept three
months without books, writing materials, communication with friends, or even a statement of charges against
him. His constitutional rights were thus violated ; the
people of Texas were outraged in the treatment of their
commissioner, besides that their humble and just petitions had been disregarded. The effect of the intelligence of these things in Texas may well be conceived :
its interests had been neglected—they were now abandoned ; the people had been oppressed—they were now
insulted. The result was increased and general irrita-
tion of feeling, and the formation of a party which
vowed eternal separation from Mexico, and which never
relaxed its efforts until Independence was declared.
That determined spirit of the Anglo-American race,
which has been the bulwark of Liberty, which has hurled
oppression from its strong-holds, and which cannòt
exist but with freedom, was now roused, and, imperious in its wrath, as mild in its mercy,—persevering in
the pursuit of its object, as omnipotent in grasping it,—
may doubtless have been carried to some extremes in
manner and in measures. And hence it probably was

that Austin, during his imprisonment in Mexico, in his communications to the people of Texas, warned them to beware of "inflammatory men, political fanatics, and political adventurers." That such there were in Texas, is admitted generally by the Texans themselves ; and that there should have been such, is no matter of wonder in a community recently formed and constantly forming, of very discordant elements, and ere yet there had been time for general unanimity of sentiment and of action. But then it should be borne in mind, that there were some of the most respectable and talented, as well as influential men of Texas, who at this time not only believed, with Austin, that Texas *might* justly provide for herself, but were disposed to *seize* at once the reigns of Government, and rid themselves of the uncertainty, if not the insecurity, of their situation.

The people of Texas generally, however, were disposed to peace, preferring to endure grievances, though great, in the hope of ultimate redress in a peaceable way, rather than risk the loss of every thing by a collision with the General Government. Gen. Austin, in all his letters from Mexico, though he expressed the opinion that the oppressive acts of the Mexican Government, considered in connection with the revolutionary state of the interior of the Republic, and the absolute want of a local Government in Texas, would justify the people in organizing of themselves a State Government ; and, if opposed in separating themselves from Mexico, yet aware that a great majority of the people were in favor of peace, if not from principle, yet from interest, constantly recommended it, and in the strongest terms.

## CHAPTER III.

SCARCELY had the people of Texas heard of the difficulties and grievances brought upon them by the General Government, when they were thrown into utter anarchy and confusion by a division in the State Legislature and authorities at Monclova in July, 1834. This was caused by the collision between the President, Santa Anna, and the General Congress, on the 13th of May of the same year. One party declared for Santa Anna, chose a military officer for their governor, put themselves under the protection of the soldiery, and retired to Saltillo, where they proceeded to annul the decrees passed by the Constitutional Legislature at Monclova, from the period of its election in January, 1833. The other party remaining at Monclova, denounced the opposite faction at Saltillo as unconstitutional. The people of Texas expected to find a remedy for the anarchy necessarily resulting from this state of things, in the approaching constitutional elections of State representatives and officers for the years 1835 and '6. That period, however, passed under the disputed authority of two governors. Now, in the early part of the year 1835, many who had before been in favor of peace, lest anarchy should be perpetual, began to speak openly of the necessity of separating themselves from Coahuila. The people of Coahuila became alarmed, and called upon the Texans to assist them in council, in order to " save the country from anarchy and confu-

4

sion." The majority of the people of Texas were for
uniting with those of Coahuila in devising some plan for a
constitutional re-organization of the State Government;
and the rather, as they knew this to be the earnest desire
of Austin, who had, moreover, by this time informed
them that the General Government had at length " remedied the evils complained of in Texas, and which threatened it with ruin," and that Santa Anna was friendly
to Texas. But the intelligent separatists knew very
well that the evils remedied were only of minor importance; that the great object of the mission of Austin to
Mexico had not been accomplished; that anarchy prevailed at home, for which they could expect no remedy
from the General Government, itself in anarchy; and they
too well appreciated the character of Santa Anna to
rely upon his promises. That they should view things
somewhat differently from Austin, was to be expected;
he was a prisoner, subject to the will of a despot;
they were yet free, and, confident of strength, resolved to
remain so. They therefore advised that "Texas should
immediately organize and save herself from impending
ruin;" that she should "hazard nothing, neither by petitions, which might not be answered, nor by requests,
which had been made; but promptly adopt a prudent
and least exceptionable course, hazarding as little to the
action of the General Government as possible; that as
Coahuila had withdrawn herself from Texas by her own
willing and unlawful act, Texas should abandon her to
her fate; that Texas, in so doing, would assume a position
of which neither the General, nor any other Government,
could complain."

This advice was certainly of a revolutionary character, of which the authors were, no doubt, well aware, and prepared to meet the consequences ; not so the unionists and peace party ; they were alarmed, and, in November, came out with an answer and an address to the people, well calculated to allay excitement, and which had for some months a very perceptible effect.  They called upon the opposite party to consider the impropriety and evil of inculcating measures, in a time of prosperity, which must result in loss, want, and wretchedness ; to consider that Santa Anna was favorable to Texas ; that the General Government had now listened to the petitions of the people of Texas, and removed the grievances of which they had complained ; to remember that the State Government had granted all she asked, had established trial by jury, had organized a Court specially for Texas ; that if their commissioner, as they complained, had been imprisoned, it was for recommending ultra measures ; and that rash measures, then taken in Texas, would further hazard his liberty and life ; that Texas had been relieved of all the expense of supporting the Government ; that there was now hope that the factions at Monclova and Saltillo would soon be reconciled ; and that, finally, the measures recommended were of a decidedly revolutionary character, and that they ought well to consider whether they were prepared and willing, by such measures, "heedlessly to rush forward in a course which might involve the country of their adoption in all the horrors of a civil war."

Had an ultimate and a radical change of government not been desirable or necessary to Texas, this address had been not only well calculated to allay excitement, but to result in permanent good ; but unfortunately, the evils remedied, which it enumerates, had been only partial and of minor importance; the greater evils, especially of anarchy, still continued, out of which new evils were constantly springing into existence. What, then, was the proper course for Texas to pursue? Let the reader judge. Austin was still in prison in Mexico; the constitutional General Congress of 1834, which was decidedly Republican and Federal, had been dissolved in May of that year by a military order of the President, before its constitutional term had expired, and the Council of Government had been dissolved; there were still two factions in the State Legislature, and the General Government was rapidly verging to a despotism under Santa Anna.

This state of things continued in Mexico until the final consolidation of a Central Government by a decree of the 3d of October, 1835; and in Texas, until a meeting of the newly elected Legislature in March of the same year. The meeting of this Legislature had been protracted from January till March by the continuation of the same difficulties which had existed since July, 1834. No sooner had this Legislature assembled, than a law was proposed for the sale of 411 leagues of land in Texas. The Congress of Mexico had intelligence of this; and denying the right of the State Legislature to sell the land, except in favor of the General Government, on the ground that the State of Coahuila and Texas was in arrears for her proportion of the national debt, not yet paid, proceeded to pass a law authorizing the national Executive to purchase the land of that State, and turn it to the account of her debt to the General Government. This did not answer the purpose of the State Legislature : it wanted money to defray its own expenses, and accordingly proceeded to pass the proposed law. Speculators were present at Monclova to purchase the land ; among them, unfortunately, were Texans, and they were the principal purchasers ; and upon them, and, through them, upon the people of Texas generally, has fallen the odium of this great land speculation. The few citizens of Texas who were engaged in this speculation, were undoubtedly much in fault ; but the fact is not generally known, that the principal fault of this, as well as other *partial* and odious, if not unconstitutional, sales of the public domain of Texas, is to be charged to the people of Coahuila, and not to those of Texas. Coahuila, by her preponderance in the State Legislature, had almost entire jurisdiction over the public domain of Texas ; hence, and because she had little public land of her own, she was opposed to the separation of Texas. Before that separation should take place, she wished to sell, and did, from time to time, sell large tracts of Texas land—generally in 11 league tracts—to her own citizens, that they might resell, and better their condition.

Military force was the order of the day in Mexico. When the sale of the 411 leagues of land was announced, Santa Anna was near by, quelling an insurrection, or rather destroying the constitutional rights and liberty of the people, in Zakatecas. Cos, commandant general of the Eastern provinces, was ordered on from Matamoras with a force to disperse the obnoxious Legislature at Monclova. This he did, and imprisoned several of the members and the governor of the State.

4*

The Texan land-speculators made their way home in all haste. They proclaimed war, separation, and independence.

The people of Texas, alarmed at the encroachments of the General, and the illegal acts of the State Government, were thrown into a most lamentable state of uncertainty, excitement, and disorder. The war party, newly combined, excited and strengthened, resorted to arms, and raised, on the 16th of August, 1835, the first standard on the plains of San Jacinto, where the conflict with Mexico, now to begin, was destined to end. From thence they marched to Anahuac, and took forcible redress of grievances there in relation to the customs. The peace party was also up and organized, and resorted to committees, and circulars, and addresses, to allay the storm. Vain attempt! as well oppose straws to the whirlwind. They were yet, however, a large as well as respectable party; and by means of their Political Chief, they addressed the people, deprecating the late acts as uncalled for, and lamenting that the interests of a majority of a people, disposed to peace, should be hazarded by the rashness of a few; representing that official communications just received from Gen. Cos, as also from the Political Chief at Bexar, breathed nothing but peace and harmony; assuring the Colonists that "they had nothing to fear;" and that "the authorities of Mexico had never thought of trampling on the rights lawfully acquired by the settlers, who ought not to doubt the Supreme Government would attend to their representations, and omit no means for promoting the welfare of all the inhabitants of the Republic;" representing, also, that there was now a reasonable prospect of obtaining a State Government in a peaceable way, since assurance had been received that Santa Anna was in favor of the same. They declared that they would promote, by every means, union, moderation, and adherence to the laws and constitution of the land ; that they would discountenance the conduct and acts of any set of individuals, less than a majority, calculated to involve Texas in a conflict with the General Government ; that they would assist that Government against those who would not obey the revenue laws, and would invite the supreme Executive to carry them into effect, suggesting such modifications as to insure the collection of duties ; that they wished to be considered faithful citizens of Mexico, and to discharge their duties as such ; that every act tending to interrupt the harmony and good understanding, existing between the General Government and Texas, deserved the marked disapprobation of every friend of good order and constitutional regularity ; and that, finally, they pledged themselves, their property, their honor, and their lives, to abide, to stand by, and to fulfil, all and every duty required of them.

Such were the professions and declarations of the peace party ; and they were undoubtedly sincere, for, though ready, as they subsequently showed themselves, to take up arms, and to oppose unconstitutional and lawless force, when apparent and certain, and aimed at themselves, yet, not having been convinced that such force *had* been exerted to their prejudice,—owing to the views they entertained of all that had transpired at Monclova,—and not considering it certain that such force *would* be exerted, owing to late representations

they had received from Mexico, in reference to the disposition particularly of Santa Anna,—they thought it
best to remain quiet, hoping for redress in a peaceable
way.*   Circumstances, however, soon compelled them
to change their minds.

* See Appendix, No. 4.

## CHAPTER IV.

WITH the events alluded to in the last chapter, begin the more immediate causes which, in October, 1835, impelled the people of Texas again to take up arms in defence of their rights. From this time, more particularly, the actions of that people have become a part of the history of mankind : "millions have sympathized in their struggles," and "nations have admired their achievements." But as all that is great and good, has been reviled, so have the motives of the people of Texas for engaging in a war, and their actions in prosecuting a war, with Mexico. In attempting to vindicate these motives, and rightly to set forth before the world these actions, the writer feels that he is incurring a great weight of responsibility ; but, conscious of desiring to exhibit only fact and truth, he is willing to meet it.

The first event alluded to as resulting in the crisis mentioned, was the high-handed proceeding of Capt. Thompson, of the Mexican navy, near Galveston, in the months of August and September, 1835.

So soon as Gen. Cos heard of the late affair at Ana-huac, he ordered Capt. Thompson to proceed from Matamoras with a sloop of war, round to Galveston, to ascertain the facts of the difficulty at Anahuac, and report to him. Thompson transcended his orders—attacked and captured an American vessel in the Texas trade. This act of aggression, whether considered or not, by the Texans, as the commencement of hostilities on the part of Mexico, had much the same effect in irritating the public mind.

But the event which, more than any thing else, operated to change the public sentiment in Texas, was the arrival of their respected commissioner, Stephen F. Austin, early in September, 1835. A man of great firmness and candor, of tried integrity, and of a sound judgment, and, by his long residence in Mexico, well acquainted with the leading events of the Revolution going on there, and best able to judge in what form of government that Revolution would terminate, the people of Texas very naturally, and with the best reason, looked to him for advice in the existing emergency. After a careful survey of the attitude in which Texas then stood to the National Government, and examination of evidence lately received in Texas of the hostile intentions of that Government, Gen. Austin addressed his fellow-citizens assembled at Brazoria, on the 8th of September, to the following effect :—I hoped to have found Texas in peace and tranquillity, but regret to find it in commotion, all disorganized, all in anarchy, and threatened with immediate hostilities. This state of things is lamentable, and a great misfortune˙; but it is one which has not been produced by any acts of the people of this country, but is the natural and inevitable consequence of the Revolution which has extended to all parts of Mexico, and of the imprudent and impolitic measures both of the General and State Governments with respect to Texas. The people here are not to be blamed; being the cultivators of the soil, they are pacific from interest, from occupation, and inclination. They have uniformly endeavored to sustain the constitution and the public quiet by pacific means ; and have not deviated from their duty as Mexican citizens. If acts of imprudence have been committed by individuals, they resulted from the revolutionary state of the whole nation, the imprudent and censurable conduct of the State authorities, and the total want of a local government in Texas. It is, indeed, a matter of surprize, and source of creditable congratulation, that so few acts of the kind have occurred under the peculiar circumstances of the times. The people of Texas, not having originated or participated in the Revolution in Mexico, their consciences and their hands are free from censure, and clean. That Revolution is now drawing to a close ; the object is to change the form of government—destroy the Federal Constitution of 1824, and establish a Central or Constitutional Government ; the States are to be converted into provinces. Will this act annihilate all the rights of Texas, and subject her to uncontrolled and unlimited dictation ? If so, ought the people of Texas to agree to this change, and surrender all or any part of their constitutional and vested rights ? These are questions of vital importance, and demand, in my opinion, a general consultation of the people. Santa Anna, as well as other influential men in Mexico, have declared to me that they are the friends of the people of Texas, and wish their prosperity, and will do all they can to promote it ; and that, in the new constitution, they will use their influence to give to Texas a special organization, suited to their education, habits, and situation. These declarations afford another rea-

son for a general consultation, that the people may de-
termine what organization will suit their education,
habits, and situation.   Such a crisis has arrived, as to
bring it home to the judgment of every man, that something m ust be done.   The constitutional rights of
Texas ought to be maintained ; and, jeopardized as
they are, demand a general consultation of the people.

This advice of Austin worked like leaven ; the people rapidly came over in sentiment to the rescue of
their rights.   This movement was greatly accelerated
by another of the exciting causes already alluded to,
which operated to bring about a change in the public
sentiment.   Soon after the publication of the address
of Gen. Austin, intelligence was received of an order
from Cos, then at Bexar, for the forcible arrest
of certain citizens of Texas, particularly Lorenzo de
Zavala.   This gentleman had sought an asylum in
Texas, from the persecutions of the existing administration in Mexico.   His offence was unknown, except
that he was the known friend of free institutions.
This man, the authorities in Texas were required, by
a military mandate, to surrender into the hands of
Gen. Cos ; who, in his zeal to secure his person, had
addressed an order to Col. Ugartechea, commandant
at Bexar, to march into the Colonies and *take* him, at
the risk of losing all the force he should employ.   The
deserts, however, neither of Zavala nor of the other
citizens, whose surrender was ordered, was with the
people of Texas a question.   They believed that the order had been given in a total disregard of their constitutional rights, and that they were bound not to obey
it.   They believed that the issuing a military mandate,

for the arrest in any manner of a citizen of Texas, would have been a disrespect to the citizens generally ; but that the issuing an order which was to be forcibly executed, and at all hazards, was an outrage upon the civil authorities of the country and upon the Constitution. The next and last of the leading causes alluded to, was an order received from Gen. Cos in the course of the month of September, requiring the citizens of Brazoria, Columbia, Velasco, and other places, to deliver up their arms to the Mexican authorities : thus attempting to carry out in Texas the plan adopted by Santa Anna, and put in execution in many parts of Mexico, of disarming those whom he suspected of being disaffected to his Government. This, with the last mentioned cause, showed the people of Texas what sort of government they were to expect—that of the bayonet, and the entire sway of the military.

By the operation of these causes, the people of Western Texas, during the month of September, became almost unanimous in favor of maintaining their rights. The plan adopted was, " to insist on their rights under the Federal Constitution of 1824, and the law of the 7th of May of that year, and union with Mexico." They re-organized, and established committees of safety and vigilance; of which the one at San Felippe de Austin was the centre of influence, where Gen. Austin was in person, watching every movement in the country, and carefully weighing every rumor from abroad.

On the 19th, this committee issued a circular, informing the people that intelligence of the most unquestionable character had been received, that Gen. Cos, who was to have left Matamoras on the 1st instant, was

5

expected at Bexar by the 16th, with 400 men, and "a battalion of Lancers close at his heels"; that the committee, from all it had learned of the disposition of Gen. Cos, as well as of the authorities in Mexico, believed that any attempt at conciliatory measures with that officer would be in vain; that nothing but the ruin of Texas was resolved upon; and that, for the people, there was now no resource but that of War! Lamentable! and, for Texas, fearful alternative!—but the decree may be said now to have gone forth, and war with Mexico to have been declared, though of defence and not aggression.   The committee, therefore, recommended the organization of the militia in the different municipalities, and the assembling of delegates of the people in consultation.

Some time previous to the publication of this circular, a demand had been made by Col. Ugartechea for a piece of ordnance which had been unconditionally given by the State Government to the citizens of De Wit's Colony for their defence.   Believing that the demand was made only as a pretext for a sudden inroad and attack upon the Colony, the people refused to give it up.   In consequence, expecting that Ugartechea would send a force against them, they, on the 25th, wrote to their fellow-citizens of Austin's Colony, informing them of what had transpired, and requesting their assistance.

Five days subsequent they again wrote, informing the people at San Felippe that a detachment of about 200 Mexican troops had arrived on the 20th, and were encamped opposite Gonzales, and that an attack was immediately expected.

About the same time, intelligence was received at
San Felippe, that the Alcalde of Goliad had been pub-
licly whipped by a Mexican officer, for not being able
to get carts in readiness so soon as they were wanted
to transport the Mexican arms on to Bexar; that the
soldiers on their march to the same place had said it
would be but a short time until they should visit the Colonists, and help themselves to what cash and other
things they had; and that the officers had declared,
that as soon as Gen. Cos reached Bexar, it would be the
signal of a march upon San Felippe.   This intelligence
was confirmed by a communication from Bexar, stat-
ing that it was the purpose of Cos to march into the
Colonies, and regulate the land affairs and other things
by military force.

On the receipt of intelligence of these things, a call
was made by the committee at San Felippe for volunteers to move on West.  At the same time, the committee, in order to acquaint the people more fully with the
aspect of the times, issued, on the 3d of October, another circular, enclosing an official letter from the Minister of Interior Relations in Mexico to the municipality of Gonzales.   This letter was to the following
effect :—" The General Congress, taking into consideration the reforms of the Constitution which have been
unanimously requested by almost all the towns of the
Republic, that august body will bear in mind the wants
of Texas, for the purpose of providing a remedy; and
the Government will cheerfully co-operate in that object, by making propositions which may best conduce to
so laudable an end, relying always on the good sense
and docility of the Colonists, who, in adopting this for

their country, subjected themselves to the alterations
which, respecting the institutions, a majority of the
nation may think proper to agree upon; which disposition the Government is decided on supporting, as also
of protecting the lovers of order, and punishing those
who foment sedition."

What, asked the committee, are the reforms spoken
of by the Minister? What can they be but the reduc-
tion of the militia of the States to "one militia-man
for every five hundred inhabitants, and the disarming
all the rest"? What but the destruction of the Constitution of 1824, and the substitution of a military, eccle-
siastical despotism? And what is the majority spoken
of by the Minister of Relations? What but the military power which has assumed the voice of the nation?
And moreover they asked,—much in the spirit and language of the patriots of '76,—if the Government of
Mexico is sincere in its professions in favor of Texas,
why all this preparation for a military invasion? Why
has Gen. Cos marched with all the disposable force
at Matamoras to Bexar? Can it be that the Government, in its fatherly care for Texas, fears that there are
those in this country who are opposed to liberal guarantees? Or are the promised guarantees only a pretext and a show to quiet Texas until the Government
is prepared to subject her to a military despotism?
The committee again exhorted their fellow-citizens to
march, as soon as possible, to the head-quarters of the
ARMY OF THE PEOPLE at Gonzales, to assist their exposed countrymen.

In the mean time, a battle had been fought near Gonzales on the morning of the 2d of October. The Mex-

ican troop, which had appeared and taken up its position on the West bank of the Guadalupe, on the 20th September, as already stated, had on the same day attempted to cross the river, and been repulsed by eighteen men. They then encamped on a neighboring mound in the prairie, where they remained until the 1st instant, when they withdrew and took a strong position some miles above Gonzales. Suspecting their object to be to wait for reinforcements, the Texans, now amounting to about one hundred and sixty men, crossed the river in the night, and marched in good order towards the enemy's encampment, near which they arrived about daylight on the 2d. After some skirmishing, Castonado, the Mexican commander, requested a conference, which was agreed to, and took place between the two armies. Castonado desired to know why he was attacked? The reply was, because he had demanded, and meant to take forcible possession of, the cannon which had been presented to the people of Gonzales for their defence, and that of the Constitution, by Constitutional authorities, and because he was acting in obedience to Santa Anna, who had destroyed both the State and Federal Constitutions. Castonado said that the cannon, which he had been ordered to demand, having been refused, he was waiting for further orders. Upon this, Col. Moore, the Texan commander, informed him that he must either surrender, join the Texans, or fight immediately. Castonado saying that he was obliged to obey orders, the conference ended and the battle began. The Texans made a spirited attack, with such admirable use of their little cannon—which vomited a shower of old iron, pieces of kettle, chain, &c., with which, in the

5*

want of better ammunition, it was charged—that the
Mexican commander showed no more desire to get
possession of it, and retreated precipitately towards
San Antonio. Several Mexicans were killed. No
Texan was injured.

## CHAPTER V.

Thus the Rubicon was passed; the war was begun. The people of Western Texas now resolved to carry that war upon the frontier, and drive every Mexican beyond the Rio Grande. They devoutly believed that the time had arrived when every good citizen should shoulder his rifle and fight for his country. They desired peace, and had avoided war; but the storm being now inevitable, they were prepared to meet it, and they said, "Let it come." The roads were thronged with citizens hurrying to the West to join the standard of their country, with the now unanimous cry, "My country, right or wrong!" Despatches were sent to the different municipalities in Eastern Texas, calling upon the people there to come to the rescue. In consequence of which, the Committees at Nacogdoches and San Augustine met and passed resolutions to raise and organize forces, and appointed their distinguished fellow-citizen, Samuel Houston, General of Department. This great man, not inexperienced in the evils of war, and contemplating the appalling odds of the conflict into which Texas had launched, lamented it as premature; yet as the die was cast, in full confidence of ultimate success, he issued a proclamation, calling on his fellow-citizens to gather around the standard of their country; informing them that the Revolution in Mexico had resulted in the creation of a

Dictator; and that Texas, having preserved its allegiance inviolate—having failed to obtain promised benefits—its constitutional rights at an end, and threatened with arbitrary power,—was compelled to assume an attitude of defence; that her only object was the attainment of national liberty, the freedom of religious opinion, and just laws.

About the same time, Lorenzo de Zavala, formerly Governor of Mexico, and late Minister to France, arrived at San Felippe, and took his seat as chairman of the committee of safety, in the place of Gen. Austin, who retired to take command of the army assembling at Gonzales. Zavala, perfectly acquainted with the whole history of Mexico, and with the character and motives of the men in power there, contributed much to enlighten and direct the public sentiment in Texas. He represented the military as the regulating power in Mexico; that the situation of the Mexican Nation was that of the greatest confusion and disorder; that certain military chiefs, at the head of whom was Santa Anna, having under them from fifteen to twenty thousand hireling soldiers, and knowing no law but that of the sword and violence, had forcibly put down all the constitutional and civil authorities; that the various acts of usurpation committed by Santa Anna, as the head of the Government, particularly the final blow aimed at the institutions of Mexico on the day of the destruction of the State Legislatures, was sufficient to destroy all claim to obedience; and that the fundamental compact having been dissolved, and all the guarantees of the civil and political rights of citizens destroyed, it was *incontestable* that Texas, and all the States of the confederation, were left to act for themselves, as circumstances might require.

Early in October, intelligence having reached New Orleans of the hostile incursion of a Mexican force upon the soil of Texas, and that its inhabitants had taken up arms in self-defence, a numerous and highly respectable meeting was held in that city for the purpose of taking into consideration the existing affairs of that country. The meeting having adopted resolutions expressing their sympathy for the people of Texas, and their determination to aid them by every means in their power, consistent with their obligations to their own Government, appointed a committee to correspond with the Provisional Government of Texas—to receive subscriptions—and to enlist volunteers in its behalf. The result was, that seven thousand dollars were soon subscribed, and two companies of volunteers enlisted, armed, and provided.

On the 8th, the important fort at Goliad, the strongest in Texas, was taken, after a short skirmish, by a small detachment of the Texan army, under the command of Captain Collinsworth. The Texans took thirty prisoners, officers and men, and about three hundred stand of arms, and stores to the amount of ten thousand dollars.

In the taking of this fort, the brave Milam acted a distinguished part. Just arrived from Mexico, where he had long been incarcerated in a dungeon, and from whence he had travelled mostly by night, obliged to hide himself by day, he fell in with the party under Captain Collinsworth, just before they had reached Goliad, overjoyed once more to meet his countrymen;

and—ready again, as always, to peril his own liberty and his life for the freedom of his country—he joined the party, and was one of the foremost in the assault upon the fort.

On the 11th, the delegates from the various municipalities, elected to form a General Council, to provide for the emergency of the times, met at San Felippe and organized.

On the same day, the army, amounting to about three hundred men, was organized at head-quarters, on the Guadalupe. Gen. Austin was elected Commander-in-Chief.

On the 13th, the army took the line of march for Bexar, with the purpose of getting possession of that important post as early as possible, and thus having in command the entire Western frontier.

On the 16th, representatives, elected to a general consultation of Texas, arrived at San Felippe, and on the evening of the same day went into committee of the whole. The members present did not constitute a quorum, a majority of the members elect having taken the field : at the request, therefore, of the absent members, and of the officers and soldiers of the army, those present adjourned until the 1st of November, having previously resolved that such of their number as could join the army, should do so, and that the rest should attach themselves to the General Council.

The army in the mean time was on the march to Bexar. In the course of this march General Austin sent a flag to Gen. Cos, then in command at Bexar. Cos refused to receive it ; and informed Gen. Austin, that if another were sent he would fire upon it. On the 20th the army reached the Salado, within five miles of Bexar, where it took a secure position, in order to wait for reinforcements. Here Gen. Austin learned that the army under Cos was busily engaged in fortify-ing San Antonio, by barricading the streets and plant-ing cannon on the top of the church, cutting down trees, and in every way exerting themselves to make a vigo-rous defence.

At the Salado, Gen. Houston, who had been elected a member to the Consultation from Nacogdoches, joined the army. He was known to but few ; but his digni-fied manner, his commanding person, and, more than all, his obvious acquaintance with military affairs, did not fail to excite the attention of the soldiers, and to gain their esteem. He remained in the army as a pri-vate soldier until his departure with the other members elect to meet in consultation at San Felippe.

Exceedingly desirous, as well as the men under his command, to march on San Antonio as soon as possible, Gen. Austin sent despatches East, requesting that rein-forcements should join him with all possible expedition.

On the 27th, a division of ninety-two men, under the joint command of Captains Fannin and Bowie—men about to be distinguished in the annals of Texas—pro-ceeded from the Salado to examine the Missions above Espada, and select the most eligible situation near Bex-ar for the encampment of the main army. Having ex-amined the sites of San Juan and San José, they pro-ceeded to a bend in the river San Antonio, near the Old Mission of Conception, where they selected a place of encampment. There was a plain in their front, and an adjoining timber, forming two sides of a triangle. In their rear was a bluff of about ten feet sudden fall, and thence a bottom extending fifty or one hundred yards to the river. In this place, in two divisions, one on each side of the triangle, they encamped for the night. Next morning an advanced guard of the enemy's cavalry appeared, and fired upon a Texan sentinel. Upon this, the Texans were called to arms, but were unable to see the enemy on account of a dense fog. When the fog disappeared, they saw themselves surrounded—that a desperate fight was inevitable, all communication with the main army being cut off. Preparations were made; the two divisions formed contiguous to each other, that either might assist the other at the shortest notice. Brush and vines, under and along the margin of the bank, were at the same time ordered to be cleared away, and at the steepest places steps to be cut for a foothold, that the soldiers might readily ascend and discharge their rifles, descend again and reload. This was scarcely done, when the engagement commenced, and soon became general. The discharge by the enemy was a continued blaze of fire, whilst that from the Texan lines was more slowly delivered, but with good aim and deadly effect. Each man, as he fired, retired under cover of the hill, to give place to others, and reload. After about ten minutes a brass four-pounder was opened upon the Texans, with a heavy discharge of grape and cannister, and a charge sounded; but the cannon was immediately cleared, and a check given to the charge. The enemy having three times repeated this experiment with the same success,—the Texans, at the same time rapidly approaching the cannon under the hill with the cry,

" The cannon and victory,"—sounded a retreat, which was most readily obeyed in a precipitate and disorderly manner.

Thus the Texans gained a complete victory over the army of the Central Government, with the loss of only one man. The loss of the enemy in killed and wounded was about one hundred. Their cannon also fell in the hands of the Texans.

In the mean time, the members elect to the Consultation, who had been with the army, had taken their departure for San Felippe, where a majority of all the members met on the 3d of November, and organized. The Hon. B. T. Archer, having been chosen President, in an able and appropriate address, suggested to the Consultation various important measures for their consideration : first, the adoption of a Declaration, setting forth to the world the reasons which had impelled the people of Texas to take up arms ; secondly, the establishment of a Provisional Government, and the election of a Governor and Lieutenant-Governor, clothed with legislative and executive powers ; and thirdly, the organization and support of the military. " You have in the field," he said, " an army, whose achievements have shed lustre on our arms. They are in want of the comforts and necessaries of life : support them, or their victories, though glorious, will result in no good. Sustain them, and they will honor you ; neglect them, and Texas is lost. Adopt a military code ; without discipline, your army will be more dangerous to itself than the enemy. There was never better material for soldiers than your army in the field ; but without discipline, they can achieve nothing. Establish military

6

laws, and, like the dragon's teeth sown by Cadmus,
they will produce armed men." He further recommended to the delegates, attention to their Indian relations, and the securing to volunteers from the United
States the rights and privileges of citizens.

The delegates then proceeded to the adoption of sun-
dry resolutions—particularly, authorizing the President
to appoint a committee to draft the proposed Declaration; for the presentation of the thanks of the delegates
to the victors at the battle of Conception; and for
other purposes.

On the 7th of November, the committee which had
been charged with the duty of drawing up a Declaration
of the reasons which impelled the people of Texas to
take up arms, reported the following, which was adopted :—

" *Whereas,* General Antonio Lopez de Santa Anna,
and other military chieftains, have, by force of arms,
overthrown the Federal institutions of Mexico, and dissolved the social compact which existed between Texas and the other members of the Mexican Confederacy,
now the good people of Texas availing themselves of
their natural rights,

## " SOLEMNLY DECLARE,

" That they have taken up arms in defence of their
rights and liberties, which were threatened by the encroachments of military despots, and in defence of the
Republican principles of the Federal Constitution of
Mexico, of 1824.

" That Texas is no longer morally or civilly bound by
the Compact of Union ; yet, stimulated by the genero-

sity and sympathy common to a free people, they offer their support and assistance to such of the members of the Mexican Confederacy as will take up arms against military despotism.

" That they do not acknowledge that the present authorities of the nominal Mexican Republic have the right to govern within the limits of Texas.

" That they will not cease to carry on war against the said authorities, whilst their troops are within the limits of Texas.

" That they hold it to be their right, during the disorganization of the Federal system and the reign of despotism, to withdraw from the Union, to establish an independent Government, or to adopt such measures as they may deem best calculated to protect their rights and liberties ; but that they will continue faithful to the Mexican Government, so long as that nation is governed by the Constitution and laws that were formed for the government of the political association.

" That Texas is responsible for the expenses of her armies, now in the field.

" That the public faith of Texas is pledged for the payment of any debts contracted by her agents.

" That she will reward by donations in land all who volunteer their services, in her present struggle, and receive them as citizens.

" THESE DECLARATIONS we solemnly avow to the world, and call God to witness their truth and sincerity, and invoke defeat and disgrace upon our heads, should we prove guilty of duplicity. "

Though, in this Declaration, the delegates pledged

their allegiance to the Mexican Government, so long as directed by the Constitution and laws, yet, in the clause "the Republican principles of the Federal Constitution," there was, in fact, an exception to that allegiance. There were parts of the Constitution of Mexico, particularly that providing for the exclusive support and toleration of the Roman Catholic religion, which were not of a Republican character. To these, the delegates did not pledge their allegiance. The clause containing this exception, was introduced and sustained by a few individuals, who, if they were not at the time in favor of a Declaration of entire Independence, believed that such a Declaration would be ultimately and ere long the necessary resort for Texas.

The expediency of the exception made was very questionable, inasmuch as it might have the effect, and probably did, of causing distrust in the minds of the Liberal party in Mexico, of the sincerity of the Texans in their alleged resort to arms in defence of their Constitutional rights. The people generally, however, were sincere to the full extent of their previous declarations; they would not yet listen to any propositions relating to a Declaration of Independence of Mexico.

On the 12th, the delegates in Consultation proceeded to elect a Governor, Lieutenant-Governor, and Council. Henry Smith was chosen Governor, and J. W. Robinson, Lieutenant-Governor. The Governor was clothed with "full and ample executive powers."

Thus had Texas now a head and a government, under which she might, with more efficiency, call forth her resources, collect and combine her energies ; and that Government being of a Constitutional character, as well as absolutely necessary to save her from anarchy, she hoped to be countenanced and sustained by the Liberal party in Mexico.

On the 13th, the committee, which had been charged with the duty, presented, in full, the plan and form of the Provisional Government, the outline of which had been previously adopted.

Gov. Smith, in a very perspicuous and forcible address, presented to the Consultation a brief sketch of the existing state and prospects of the country, and a summary of the important measures which demanded their consideration. "You have," he remarked, " to call system from chaos ; to start the wheels of Government, yet impeded by conflicting interests ; without funds, without munitions of war, with an army unprovided, and contending against a powerful foe." He recommended the granting of letters of marque and reprisal ; the organization of a corps of Rangers to protect the frontiers against the savages ; the rewarding, in a liberal manner, foreign volunteers in the service of Texas ; the sending agents to foreign countries, clothed with special powers for procuring for Texas the aid of generous foreigners ; the establishment of a tariff and the appointment of revenue officers ; the organization of the militia ; and the appointment of a postmaster-general. All which measures, subsequently, came under the consideration of the Consultation, and were adopted.

The main army—which, on the 28th, had encamped at the Mission of Conception—about the 1st of November, took up a position near San Antonio, and commenced the siege of that place.

On the 3d, a detachment from a part of the volunteer army stationed at Goliad, obtained a decisive vic-

6*

tory over a force of the enemy stationed at Lepantitlan, near San Patricio. The detachment consisted of thirty men, who fought the enemy—more than twice their number—for about thirty minutes, when the latter retreated, leaving them in possession of the field. They sustained no loss; that of the enemy, in killed and wounded, was twenty-eight.

On the 8th, a signal victory was gained over the enemy, near Bexar, by a detachment from the main army, sent out for the purpose of intercepting reinforcements to General Cos. The detachment consisted of twenty-seven men, who were attacked by a company of one hundred and sixty of the Morelos cavalry. The Texans immediately retired to a ravine, from whence they opened so deadly a fire upon the enemy, that they retreated precipitately towards San Antonio, with the loss of five killed and several wounded. The Texans sustained no loss.

## CHAPTER VI.

IN the siege of Bexar, Gen. Austin adopted the Fabian system of delay. He deemed it best to "waste away the resources, and spirits, and numbers of the enemy, by a protracted siege, the ultimate success of which appeared certain, without any serious hazard." This policy did not suit the volunteers. They had left their homes in warm weather, with only their summer clothing, expecting that Bexar would be taken in two or three weeks. The cold and rainy season had now set in, which was more than usually inclement; they were suffering much for want of provisions, as well as clothing. In this situation, their term of volunteer service having more than expired, they were on the point of breaking up and returning to their homes. This was prevented, as regarded the greater number, by the timely intelligence from Government, that all who would remain in the army until the fall of Bexar should receive twenty dollars per month.

On the 25th, General Austin, having intelligence of his appointment as Commissioner to the United States, left the army, and retired to San Felippe. Edward Burleson was chosen to succeed him in command. Gen. Burleson adopted the plan of Austin, and protracted the siege. The volunteers were daily departing to their homes, and but few arrived; it was necessary to devise some measure to keep them together. About the 30th, the officers adopted the following plan :—

They ordered a general parade, formed the volunteers
into a hollow square, addressed them in an eloquent
manner upon the great importance of persevering in
the siege, and requested such as were willing to
remain thirty days, or until the fall of Bexar, to
signify the same by advancing some paces in front.
The plan succeeded; most pledged themselves to remain. But, tired of inaction and delay, they demanded
an immediate assault on the town. A day was, therefore, appointed; that day passed without any movement,
and the succeeding day was appointed; which having
also passed in inaction, the Commander-in-Chief gave
orders for a retreat on the evening of the next day, the
4th of December, to Gonzales, to winter quarters. This
retreat had accordingly commenced at the appointed
time, when, by good fortune, the Texan arms, about to
suffer a temporary eclipse, if not dishonor, were turned
to victory and to glory.

Just at the critical time of its departure, a Mexican deserter rode up to the army, from San Antonio,
who informed the Texans that there were many disaffected troops under Gen. Cos, opposed to the military
government of Santa Anna; and that San Antonio might
be easily taken. On the receipt of this intelligence,
two hundred and fifty of the volunteers immediately resolved to attack the town, and chose Benjamin R. Milam, the hero of many a bloody fray and hazardous
adventure, to lead them on. Milam determined upon a
plan of attack worthy of his character as a soldier.
The city of San Antonio, on the West side of the river
of the same name, is in the form of an oblong square.
On the East side of the river, nearly opposite, and communicating with the town by two small bridges, was a

strong fort, the Alamo. The volunteers were on the West side of the town. At three o'clock on the morning of the 5th, Milam ordered Col. Neil, with a company of artillery, to proceed round by the source of the river San Antonio to the Alamo, and make a feint upon it, for the purpose of drawing the attention of the Mexicans that way, whilst he, with the main force, should enter the town on the West. Col. Neil, accordingly, reached the Alamo about day-light, and opened a brisk fire upon it, and Milam at the same time entered San Antonio from the opposite direction. Neil, according to previous orders, when, from the firing in the town, he saw that Milam had possession, retraced his steps, and also entered from the West, without loss, though exposed to a raking fire of the enemy. Confident of security, the Mexicans were taken entirely by surprize— some even in their beds.

But the city was yet to be taken ; it had only been entered, and the work was of immense magnitude. The buildings were of stone, strong, and many of them fortified, especially those about the public square, where Gen. Cos had entrenched himself with the greatest possible care, by making a strong breast-work in each opening ; by cutting a fosse or trench about eight feet deep ; by sinking two rows of piles about six feet apart, filling the interstices with earth taken from the trench ; and by tying the tops of the piles with raw hide ropes. At each of the places so fortified, there was a piece of artillery stationed, and completely masqued, having a roof over it, and a small opening for the muzzle of the gun left in the breast-work. In addition to this, upon an ancient church in the centre of the public square, was planted artillery, at an elevation of about sixty feet, which commanded the whole town and surrounding country. With all these formidable obstacles had the volunteers to contend, and also with more than three times their number of the choice troops of Mexico. At 7 o'clock, a heavy cannonading from the town was seconded by a well directed fire from the Alamo. In consequence of which the Texans were unable to use their artillery, and confined to a close but well aimed fire from their rifles, which obliged the enemy, notwithstanding their advantageous position, to slacken their fire, and several times to abandon their artillery within the range of the Texan rifles. The loss of the Texans during the day was one private killed ; Col. Ward and a first lieutenant severely wounded. During the whole night, the Texans labored in opening trenches and strengthening their position. On the morning of the 6th, the enemy, protected by parapets, opened a brisk fire from the tops of some houses which they had occupied in front of the Texans, accompanied by a cannonading from both the town and the Alamo. Notwithstanding, the Texans gained considerable advantage during the day ; their loss was three privates, badly wounded. On the 7th, the enemy opened a heavy fire from their batteries, which, in the course of the day, was silenced by the superior fire of the Texans. On this day fell the brave, the lamented Milam, shot in the head.

On the morning of the 8th, having lost their leader, many of their officers being wounded, exhausted by three days' constant exertion, and by want of food, the principal part of their work yet to be done, and of appalling magnitude, the assailants were all but disheartened. The fortified public square had not yet been reached, and the buildings upon the side of it in the direction of the approach of the Texans, were remote from those in the rear, and filled with soldiers, who, from loop-holes cut in the walls, could pour a most deadly fire on their assailants. But great as was the danger, there were not wanting daring spirits full willing to encounter it —to brave the muzzles of the enemy's guns, in order to attain their object. Accordingly, on the night of the 9th, when a flying cloud obscured the full orbed moon, they rushed in the direction of the square, reached the point of attack unperceived, broke into the fortified buildings, drove the enemy out, took possession of their guns without the loss of a man, fired upon them in the public square, and drove them from thence across the river into the Alamo.

The conflict had continued four days, during all which time there had been waving from the Alamo, in proud defiance, the national, and also a black and red flag, in vain token of " no quarter" ; yet, on the morning of the 9th, a white flag appeared, and conditions of cap- itulation were submitted to the Texans ! For these it was stipulated that Gen. Cos and his officers, with their arms and private property, should retire into the inte- rior of the Republic, on parole of honor that they would not in any way oppose the re-establishment of the Fed- eral Constitution ; that they should take with them all the Mexican convicts, cavalry, and a part of the infan- try, the remaining troops being at liberty to depart or not, as they pleased ; and that all public property, mo- ney, and munitions of war, should be delivered over to the Texans.*

* See Appendix, No. 5.

## CHAPTER VII.

THUS had the Texans achieved a most important conquest, and driven each hostile vagabond Mexican beyond the Rio Grande.

On the 12th inst. Gen. Houston, appointed Major General and Commander-in-Chief of the army of Texas, issued his proclamation to the people.\*    Soon after, having visited Refugio and Goliad, for the purpose particularly of superintending the formation of a regiment at the latter place under Col. Fannin, he departed on furlough to Nacogdoches, to treat with Indians in that neighborhood.

The General Council of the Provisional Government in the mean time, since its organization on the 12th of November, had exerted itself in a very creditable manner to protect and sustain the country, and particularly to provide for the volunteer army in the field ; it had appointed to the chief command of that army an able general ; had provided for the raising a regular army ; for establishing and organizing a corps of rangers ; for the establishment of a navy ; for the regulation of the militia ; for the purchase of provisions, arms, &c.; and for other purposes.    It had appointed able commissioners to proceed to the United States of the North, to solicit aid and assistance in behalf of Texas ; and had

* See Appendix, No. 6.

now, at the close of the campaign at Bexar, under consideration the calling a Convention of the people. This
was at the instance of Gen. Austin, who had arrived at
San Felippe on the 29th inst. and had advised the calling of a Convention for reasons which will presently
appear.

Though the late achievements of the Texan arms
had been signal and vast, considering the odds opposed, though the political and moral effect of those
achievements was about to be as salutary as they had
been brilliant ; to inspire confidence at home, as well
as admiration abroad ; yet it was evident that the work
which the people of Texas had taken in hand was but
begun ; that one act only of her tragedy had been performed ; and that others of great, if not of fearful interest, were about to be evolved.    At this time had been
published in Texas the decree of the General Congress
of Mexico of the 3d of October, which had put an end
to the Federal system.    Before this, the people of
Texas had known only that the Central party was in
power in Mexico, and that the obvious tendency of its
acts was the establishment of a Central Military Government.    Now it was known, and published to the
world, that the Federal Government and Constitution
were, in effect, annihilated.    What course, therefore,
should the people of Texas now pursue ?    Should they
battle alone for the re-establishment of the Federal Constitution and Government, after almost every voice in
their favor had been silenced in Mexico ?    It were an
hopeless undertaking.  Should they consent to hang a remote territorial appendage to the Central Government,
governed by a " military officer and a bishop ?"  Impossi-

7

ble. Should they lay down their arms, and return to peaceful avocations, in the hope of peace and security ? They knew full well that the Government of Mexico would not cower at its reverses; that it would make every exertion to regain its laurels lost, to plant its standard in the heart of Texas, and "punish the rebels." What possible consistent course, then, was left, but to declare entire independence of Mexico, and "fight it out ?" Many of the more intelligent of the people now saw this, the only alternative; and believing that the provisional character of the existing Government was inadequate to the adoption of so responsible a measure, they, and particularly Gen. Austin, recommended a resort to the people anew, in the calling a General Convention.    In compliance with this advice, there was passed by the Provisional Government, on the 10th of December, an ordinance and decree for calling a Convention.

Though darkness was now gathering in the West, yet light was breaking in from the East upon the affairs of Texas, and upon every gale was wafted the cheering voice of friends and of brothers.    Not only in Louisiana, but in Tennessee, in Alabama, in Georgia, and in other States, volunteer companies had been enrolled and money subscribed in aid of Texas.    The chivalry of the South and West was roused and impatient to rush upon her plains.    Already had the "New Orleans Greys," and other volunteer companies from the States, won immortal honor in the fall of Bexar.    On the 17th of November, the citizens of Nashville, Tennessee, had convened, passed spirited resolutions, and opened a subscription and a list for volunteers in aid of Texas; on which occasion one munificent individual subscribed five thousand dollars. On the 25th December, the chivalrous Fannin, who had already gained laurels, and a name, enviable in Texas, had the satisfaction of greeting his countrymen and fellow-citizens of the Georgia volunteers, rejoicing that the question, " Where are your Georgia volunteers ?" was at length answered by " the shrill sound of the fife, the soul-stirring beat of the drum, and the flash of the bright sun on the rifles" of the Georgia battalion.

About the same time a company of volunteers, of the most respectable families of Alabama, was enrolled at Courtland in that State, and marched for Texas under the command of Dr. Shackleford. On the eve of their departure, assembled amidst a large concourse of their fellow-citizens, they were addressed in a manner of pathos and feeling interest, which left not a dry eye in the assembly ; the blessing of Heaven was implored on them and the cause in which they had embarked, and they left with benedictions and amidst cheers choked with sobs. A more disinterested, chivalrous set of men never took up arms to relieve the oppressed. They landed on the coast of Texas at the most inclement season of the year, where no provisions could be found ; they subsisted two weeks upon game alone—a part of the time even upon wolves—and then, when opportunity offered, proffered their services to the Government of Texas, to assist in the defence of its soil, if they were needed—if not, they were prepared to depart as they came, at their *own* expense.

This chivalrous and generous spirit, which was not confined to one, but common to all the companies of volunteers in the cause of Texas, is as creditable to that cause as to those who thus sustained it, and is enough to wipe off forever the vile aspersions which have been lavished upon it.

Notwithstanding the reasons which have been mentioned for a Declaration of Independence, the popular mind in Texas was not yet prepared for that measure, but disposed rather to abide by their oaths and the Constitution, in the hope of some favorable change in Mexico. It was, therefore, towards the close of the month of December, resolved, with the sanction of the General Council, to strike boldly at the Central Government, and to carry the war beyond the Rio Grande. This the Texans had resolved upon, with the expectation of exciting the Liberals of Mexico to unite with them in re-establishing, on Mexican soil, the banners of Morales and Hidalgo. It was proposed first to attack the enemy at Matamoras, and then, "if Heaven decreed, wherever Tyranny should raise its malignant form."

Accordingly, on the 1st of January, two hundred volunteers left Bexar under Col. Grant, and proceeded to Goliad. Their intention was to have marched from this point to Matamoras; but the larger part of them, losing confidence in their commander—having been told his object was plunder—left him, and joined the force at Goliad. Grant, with about fifty of his party, who adhered to him, and about twenty men under Col. Johnson, who subsequently joined him, proceeded on the 20th inst. towards Matamoras, with the avowed purpose of driving in horses and cattle. The result was, that, having separated in two parties, and each having got possession of what cattle and horses they wanted, on their return they fell in with a part of Santa Anna's army,—one party, under Johnson, at San Patricio, where they were, all but two, (Johnson and another individual,) cut off; the other party, under Grant, at Aqua Dulce, where they were suddenly attacked whilst watering their horses and cattle, and cut off to a man.

But the question of a Declaration of Independence had now become one of absorbing interest. The opponents of the measure maintained, that, so long as the Federal Constitution was in existence, the people of Texas were bound by their oaths of allegiance to it; and that so long as there were Liberals in Mexico, who, influenced by their appeals and gallant bearing, had staked life and property in support of the Federal system, they were bound to aid them; that Texas, with a population of only sixty thousand, already burthened with a debt of five hundred thousand dollars, and without a dollar in her treasury, would, by a Declaration of Independence, involve herself in a war with all Mexico, which might last for years, during which she would have to maintain a standing army and foreign relations, which would cost her millions of money, and that for all this she had no resources; that the idea of Independence, therefore, was madness. On the other hand, the advocates of the measure maintained, first, that the people of Texas had, morally and politically, the right to declare their Independence; that Governments are bound as well as subjects, and that if the one violate their engagements, the other are discharged from their allegiance; that Santa Anna, having by

7*

force of arms overthrown the Federal institutions of Mexico, and dissolved the social compact which had existed between Texas and the other members of the confederacy, Texas was no longer, morally or politically, bound by that compact ; that the doctrine of the reciprocal obligations of the governor and the governed, is an elemental part of national law, recognized and enforced by all the standard writers on that law ; and that the same doctrine was at the foundation of the English Revolution in 1688, which banished the Stuart family from the throne ; for which, the reason assigned by the British Parliament in declaring the abdication of James the Second, was, "that King James the Second" has "endeavored to subvert the Constitution of the kingdom by breaking the original compact between King and people." Secondly, they maintained that it was expedient to declare Independence; that Texas, placed between the Sabine and the Rio Grande, on the threshold of the Mexican gulf, with a long line of sea coast, a soil rich in all the productions of the South, and intersected by numerous rivers, had within herself all the elements of prosperity and means of greatness, with a distinct political orbit to move in, assigned her by the God of Nature himself; that by a Declaration of Independence, Texas would have the advantage of "full power to levy war, contract alliances, establish commerce, and do all other acts which independent States may of right do ;" that the late achievements of their volunteer army, under all the discouraging circumstances, with the countenance and aid they were receiving from the United States, was a pledge to the people of Texas of their ability to establish and maintain their Independence; and, finally, they maintained, that in a comparison, in most important particulars, of the causes which should induce the people of Texas to declare Independence, with those assigned by the people of the British Colonies for their Declaration of Independence, the former would appear to be the greater and more urgent; that the people of those Colonies complained that the King of Great Britain had " dissolved their representative houses"—the people of Texas, that Santa Anna had turned their Legislature out of doors, and imprisoned its members; that those Colonies complained that the King had kept among them, "in times of peace, standing armies"—the people of Texas, that the Central Government, under Santa Anna, had done the same among them, and demanded their arms; that the former complained that their valuable laws and forms of government had been fundamentally altered—the latter, that Santa Anna had trampled on all law, and destroyed their form of government; that the former maintained that the King had virtually abdicated his government in the Colonies by declaring war against them—the latter, that Santa Anna, a usurper and a tyrant, as well as a fomenter of war against the people of Texas, had no possible claim to their allegiance.

But doubts and discussions in respect of a Declaration of Independence were soon ended by information received from Mexico, that all parties there had united in opposition to Texas, and that war was inevitable.

About the same time—the last of January—communications were received from their Commissioners in the United States, informing the people of Texas that they had effected a loan in New Orleans to the amount of $200,000, and that a farther loan of $50,000 was in progress; that, in their opinion, the willingness of the citizens of New Orleans to contribute large sums of money to aid the people of Texas, and the interest manifested in their behalf on the part of the citizens of the United States generally, left no doubt as to the course which Texas ought to pursue; that to contend longer for the Constitution of 1824, would do her no good, but much harm, inasmuch as it would prevent many from joining her standard who could render her most efficient service; and that, for these reasons, they, the Commissioners, recommended an *immediate Declaration of Independence.*

On the 18th of February, according to the act of the Provisional Government, the delegates to the General Convention were elected, and clothed with plenary powers. They were to assemble on the 1st day of March.

## CHAPTER VIII.

A STORM was now gathering on the Rio Grande, about to pour its desolating effects on the plains of Texas. War, with its most terrific attendants, was rolling on its crimson car, and vindictive Fury led the van : Santa Anna was coming, proclaiming death and extermination to the rebels. One thousand troops were at Matamoras, a thousand ready to cross into Texas above, a thousand more were already on the Rio Frio, and forces were rapidly gathering in all directions, destined against Texas. They were stimulated, some by hopes of revenge, some of plunder, some of *fairer game*, and all by the promise of honors, of pensions, and of liberal pay. Of these troops a large number were cavalry, the choice troops of the interior, and armed with lances, muskets, swords, and pistols. Santa Anna had sworn to gain Texas, or lose Mexico. But he was about to attack and arouse the lion in his lair— about to attack those, who, though few in numbers and weak in resources, yet mighty in spirit and in name— the sons of the conquerors of Tyranny in the Old and New World—were to roll back upon him the tide of war, and strike his myrmidons to the earth. There was about to be a contest on the soil of Texas, which, for its moral character, though not its physical, for the object at stake, was to demand the sympathy and intensest interest of the civilized world. But let us not anticipate, but introduce the struggle as it came.

The plan adopted by the invader was to strike first at Bexar and Goliad, and then march into the heart of the Colonies; Generals Sezma, Filasola, and Cos, were to lead one division on Bexar; Urrea and Garay a second against Goliad: and Santa Anna, in person, at the head of a third division, was to pass on to Bexar or Goliad, as circumstances might require. The disposable force of Texas, at this awful period, was limited almost entirely to a small garrison of one hundred and forty efficient men at Bexar, under the command of Col. Travis, and about four hundred men garrisoned at Goliad, under the command of Col. Fannin.

On the 21st of February a division of the Mexican army appeared before San Antonio, attacked and took possession of the town, drove the little Texan garrison into the Alamo, and immediately began the siege of that fort. Of the progress of the siege, which continued about two weeks, the most important information is given by the lamented Travis in his letter addressed to the people of Texas of the 24th, and in one to the Convention, dated March 3d. In the first he says:—
" I am besieged by a thousand or more Mexicans under Santa Anna. I have sustained a continual bombardment and cannonade for twenty-four hours, and have not lost a man. The enemy have demanded a surrender at.discretion, otherwise the garrison is to be put to the sword, if the fort is taken. I have answered the summons with a cannon shot, and our flag still waves proudly from the walls. I shall never surrender or retreat. Victory or death !" In his letter to the Con-

vention he says : " From the 25th to the present date, the enemy have kept up a bombardment and a heavy cannonade. They have been busily employed in encircling us with entrenched encampments on all sides. Notwithstanding all this, a company of thirty-two men from Gonzales made their way in to us on the morning of the 1st, at three o'clock, and Col. Bonham (a courier) got in this morning. I have so fortified this place, that the walls are generally proof against cannon balls, and I still continue to entrench on the inside, and strengthen the walls by throwing up the dirt. At least two hundred shells have fallen inside of our works without having injured a man ; indeed, we have been so fortunate as not to lose a man from any cause, and we have killed many of the enemy. The spirits of my men are still high, although they have had much to depress them. We have contended for ten days against an enemy whose numbers are variously estimated at from fifteen hundred to six thousand men, with Gen. Sezma and Col. Batres, the aids-de-camp of Santa Anna, at their head. A reinforcement of about two thousand men is now entering Bexar from the West, and I think it more than probable Santa Anna is in town, from the rejoicing we hear. Col. Fannin is said to be on the march to this place with reinforcements, but I fear it is not true, as I have repeatedly sent to him for aid without receiving any. Col. Bonham, my special messenger, arrived at La Bahia fourteen days ago with a request for aid ; and on the entrance of the enemy into Bexar, ten days ago, I sent an express to Col. Fannin, which arrived at Goliad next day, urging him to send us reinforcements. None have yet arrived.  I look to the Colonies alone for aid : unless it arrives soon, I shall have to fight the enemy on his own terms.   I feel confident that the determined valor and desperate courage heretofore evinced by my men will not fail them in the last struggle ; and although they may be sacrificed to the vengeance of a Gothic enemy, the victory will cost so dear, that it will be worse for him than a defeat.   God and Texas! Victory or death !"

In a letter to a friend he says :—

" I am still here, in fine spirits.   With one hundred and forty men I have held this place ten days against a force variously estimated at from fifteen hundred to six thousand ; and I shall continue to hold it till I get relief from my countrymen, or I will perish in its defence. We have had a shower of bombs andcannon balls continually falling among us the whole time, yet none of us have fallen.   We have been miraculously preserved. We had an action on the 25th ult. in which we repulsed the enemy with considerable loss : on the night of the 25th, they made another attempt to charge us in the rear of the fort ; but we received them gallantly, by a discharge of grape shot and musquetry, and they took to their scrapers immediately.   They are now encamped under entrenchments, on all sides of us.      *        *

" All our couriers have gotten out without being caught, and a company of thirty-two men from Gonzales got in two nights ago ; and Col. Bonham got in to-day, by coming between the powder-house and the enemy's encampment.      *        *        *        *        *

Let the Convention go on and make a Declaration of Independence ; and we will then understand, and the

world will understand, what we are fighting for.  If Independence is not declared, I shall lay down my arms,
and so will the men under my command.  But under
the flag of Independence, we are ready to peril our lives
a hundred times a day, and to dare the monster who is
fighting us under a blood-red flag, threatening to mur-
der all prisoners and to make Texas a waste desert.
I shall have to fight the enemy on his own terms ; yet I
am ready to do it, and if my countrymen do not rally to
my relief, I am determined to perish in the defence of
this place, and my bones shall reproach my country for
her neglect.   With five hundred men more, I will drive
Sezma beyond the Rio Grande, and I will visit vengeance on the enemies of Texas, whether invaders or
resident Mexican enemies.   All the citizens that have
not joined us, are with the enemy fighting against us.
Let the Government declare them public enemies, otherwise she is acting a suicidal part.   I shall treat them
as such, unless I have superior orders to the contrary.
My respects to all friends, and confusion to all ene-
emies.   God bless you."

This was the last ever heard from the lamented
Travis, or any of his compatriots in arms.  They sold
their lives as dearly as possible, and fell to a man.
Thus fall the brave, when the spirit of Liberty nerves
them to the conflict !

As every thing relating to this memorable siege
must be interesting, I will insert a brief abstract from
the journal of Almonte, an aid of Santa Anna, commencing with the 27th of February, three days subsequent to the date of Travis' first letter :—

" Saturday, 27th.—Lieut. Menchard was sent with a
8

party of men for corn, cattle, and hogs, to the farms of Seguin and Flores. It was determined to cut off the water from the enemy on the side next to the old mill. There was little firing from either side during the day. The enemy worked hard all day to repair some entrenchments. In the afternoon the President was observed by the enemy and fired at. In the night a courier was despatched to Mexico, informing the Governor of the taking of Bexar.

"28th.—News was received that a reinforcement of two hundred was coming to the enemy by the road from La Bahia. The cannonading was continued.

"29th.—In the afternoon the battalion of Allende took post at the East of the Alamo. The President reconnoitered. At midnight Gen. Sezma left the camp with the cavalry of Dolores and the infantry of Allende, to meet the enemy coming from La Bahia to the aid of the Alamo.

"March 1st.—Early in the morning Gen. Sezma wrote from the Mission de la Espadar, that there was no enemy, or trace of any, to be discovered. The cavalry and infantry returned to camp. At 12 o'clock the President went out to reconnoitre the mill-site to the northwest of the Alamo. Col. Ampudia was commissioned to construct more trenches. In the afternoon the enemy fired two twelve-pound shots at the house of the President, one of which struck the house.

"2d.—Information was received that there was corn at the farm of Seguin, and Lieut. Menchard, with a party, was sent for it. The President discovered in the afternoon a covered road within pistol shot of the Alamo, and posted the battalion of Ximenes there.

"3d.—The enemy fired a few cannon and musket shots at the city. I wrote to Mexico, directing my letters to be sent to Bexar—that before three months the campaign would be ended. The General-in-Chief went out to reconnoitre. A battery was erected on the north of the Alamo, within musket shot. Official despatches were received from Urrea, announcing that he had routed the colonists of San Patricio—killing sixteen, and taking twenty-one prisoners. The bells were rung. The battalions of Zapadores, Aldama, and Toluca, arrived. The enemy attempted a sally in the night at the sugar-mill, but were repulsed by our advance.

"4th.—Commenced firing very early, which the enemy did not return. In the afternoon one or two shots were fired by them. A meeting of Generals and Colonels was held. After a long conference, Cos, Castrillon, and others, were of opinion that the Alamo should bo assaulted *after* the arrival of two twelve-pounders, expected on the 7th inst. The President, Gen. Ramirez, and I, were of opinion that the twelve-pounders should not be waited for, but the assault made. In this state things remained, the General not coming to any definite resolution."

The storming of the Alamo took place on the morning of the 6th, the second after the conference of the Mexican officers. The events of that memorable morning, on which was exhibited perhaps the most obstinate and determinate valor ever known, have been but very partially related, since not an American belonging to the fort—except a woman, Mrs. Dickerson, and a negro man, Col. Travis' servant—was left to tell the tale. The account the most to be relied upon, and

which is undoubtedly substantially correct, is given by
a negro man, Ben, who, at the time of the siege, acted
as cook for Santa Anna and Almonte.  Ben had previously been a steward on board several American vessels—had been taken up at New-York, in 1835, by
Almonte as body servant—had accompanied him in
that capacity to Vera Cruz, and thence to Bexar.
After the fall of the Alamo he was sent, with Mrs.
Dickerson and Travis' servant, to the Texan camp at
Gonzales, and subsequently became cook to General
Houston.

"I," says a highly respectable officer of the General's Staff, "had repeated conversations with Ben relative to the fall of the Alamo.  He knew but little.  He
stated that Santa Anna and Almonte occupied the
same house in the town of Bexar, and that he cooked
for both ; that, on the night previous to the storming
of the fort, Santa Anna ordered him to have coffee
ready for them all night ; that both he and Almonte
were conversing constantly, and did not go to bed ;
that they went out about midnight, and about two or
three o'clock returned together to the house ; that
Santa Anna ordered coffee immediately, threatening
to run him through the body if it was not instantly
brought ; that he served them with coffee ; that Santa
Anna appeared agitated, and that Almonte remarked
'it would cost them much ;' that the reply was, 'it
was of no importance what the cost was, that it must
be done.'

"'After drinking coffee,' says Ben, 'they went out,
and soon I saw rockets ascending in different directions, and shortly after I heard musketry and cannon,

and by the flashes I could distinguish large bodies of Mexican troops under the walls of the Alamo. I was looking out of a window in the town, about five hundred yards from the Alamo, commanding a view of it. The report of the cannon, rifles, and musketry, was tremendous. It shortly died away, day broke upon the scene, and Santa Anna and Almonte returned, when the latter remarked, that 'another such victory would ruin them.' They then directed me to go with them to the fort, and point out the bodies of Bowie and Travis—whom I had before known—which I did. The sight was most horrid.'"

On other authority we have it, that at day-break on the morning of the 6th, the enemy surrounded the fort with their infantry, with the cavalry forming a circle outside, to prevent the escape of the Texans. The number of the enemy was at least 4000, opposed to 140! Gen. Santa Anna commanded in person, assisted by four generals and a formidable train of artillery. The Texans were greatly exhausted by incessant toils and watchings, having sustained, for several days, a heavy bombardment and several real and feigned attacks. But American valor and love of Liberty displayed themselves to the last: they were never more conspicuous. Twice did the enemy apply to the walls their scaling ladders, and twice did they receive a check; for the Texans were resolved to verify the words of the immortal Travis, that he would make a "victory worse to the enemy than a defeat." A pause ensued after the second attack, which, by the exertions of Santa Anna and his officers, was again renewed, and the assailants

8*

poured in over the walls " like sheep." The struggle, however, did not end here. Unable, from the crowd and want of time, to load their guns and rifles, the Texans made use of the butt ends of the latter, and continued the fight till life ebbed out of their wounds, and the enemy had conquered the fort ; but not its brave, its matchless defenders. They perished, but yielded not. Only one remained to ask quarter, which was denied by the ruthless enemy. Total extermination succeeded, and the darkness of death closed upon the scene ! Spirits of the mighty had fallen ; but their memory shall brighten the page of Texan history ; and they shall be hailed, like the demi-gods of old, as the founders of new institutions, and the patterns of virtue !

The storming of the fort had lasted less than an hour. Col. Travis had stood on the walls cheering his men, and exclaiming " Hurra, my boys !" till he received the shot of which he fell. A Mexican officer then rushed upon him, and lifted his sword to destroy his victim, who, collecting all his expiring energies, directed a thrust at his inhuman foe, which changed their fortunes,—for the victim became the victor ; and the remains of both descended to eternal sleep—but not alike to everlasting fame.

The end of David Crocket, of Tennessee, the great hunter of the West, was as glorious as his career in life had been conspicuous. He and his companions were found with heaps of dead around them, whom they had immolated on the altar of Texan Liberty. His countenance was unchanged, and as fresh as when in his wonted exercise of the chase in the forest, or on the prairie. Texas, with pride, numbers him among the martyrs to her cause.

Major Evans, of the artillery, was shot when in the act of setting fire to a train of powder to blow up the magazine, agreeably to the previous orders of Travis. In the magazine was near a ton of powder, which, had it exploded, might have put an end to the career of Santa Anna, and blown to a more timely destruction the minions of his power, destined to whiten with their bones the plains of San Jacinto or the prairies of the West. Santa Anna, when the body of Evans was pointed out to him, drew his dirk and stabbed it twice in the breast.*

James Bowie, who was lying sick, was murdered in his bed, and his body mutilated.

The bodies of the Texans were denied the right of burial : stripped, thrown in a pile, and burned !†   Thus was bigotry added to cruelty. But revenge had already been taken : fifteen hundred Mexicans lay weltering in their blood !

---

* The account of this act was subsequently verified by the discovery of a shirt on a Mexican prisoner, which was recognized as having belonged to Evans, and which had in the bosom two cuts like those of a dirk.

† See Appendix, No. 7.

## CHAPTER IX.

In the mean time, the delegates to the General Convention had met at Washington on the 1st March, and on the 2d had passed, unanimously, a Declaration of Independence. Gen. Houston, who had been for some time East, on a furlough, treating with the Indians, had again appeared in Western Texas as a delegate to the Convention; had been re-elected, by the same, Major General and Commander-in-Chief of the Army; and had established his head-quarters at Gonzales, on the Guadaloupe, where he had in command only about 300 troops. With this small force, and not well provided with ammunition, on hearing of the disaster of the Alamo, and expecting an immediate advance of the enemy, he thought best to fall back on the Colorado, which he did on the 10th, in order to gain time for reinforcements.

At the time this retreat was determined on, and families directed to move East, orders were given that all property, which could not be removed, should be destroyed, and the abandoned country laid waste : thus both leaving the enemy no chance of supplies and a further example of the firm, determined spirit of those they had to contend against.

But though the people of Texas, now that the enemy was upon them, were generally prepared to take a firm stand, and to fight, as they soon showed themselves to

be—yet they had hitherto been exceedingly remiss—
had shown an unaccountable apathy indeed, when told
by the officers of Government that the enemy was really
approaching, and when called upon to arm and meet
him.    An exception should be made in favor of many
of the female part of the community, who, in a very creditable manner, exerted their influence, and some their
hands, to sustain their country.    But the men, for
whatever reason—it may be because they did not believe the reports of the approach of the enemy, some
reports having proved false ;  or, it may be because they
had an overweening estimation of their superiority to
that enemy—were in error and in fault, in remaining
quietly at their homes when they should have been in
the field.    But for this, and had the urgent appeals of
the Commandants at Bexar and at Goliad been listened and responded to, the former post might not now
have fallen a prey to the enemy, nor the latter been on
the brink of destruction.

Orders had now been given to Col. Fannin to abandon the fort at Goliad, and to fall back to Victoria.
These orders were not, for some reason, complied with
till it was too late : it might have been, because received at an unpropitious moment, after Col. Fannin
had unfortunately divided his forces, and whilst he
was waiting to re-unite them.    He had first, on a
representation that the enemy were at Refugio, despatched Capt. King, on the 11th, with twenty-eight
men, to convey away families from that place;
which resulted in a bloody battle on the 9th, between
the little force under King and eleven hundred of the
enemy, in an open prairie ; and in the subsequent sur-

render of King and his men, after that, taking refuge in the church of the Mission, they had most heroically sustained themselves against the whole force of
the enemy for three days : they then, because their ammunition had failed, surrendered, and were taken out
and shot ! Their bones yet whiten the prairie. Again,
Col. Fannin, not having heard from King—as the despatches of the latter were intercepted by the enemy—
had sent out a second detachment—Col. Ward and his
battalion—as a reinforcement to King. This resulted
in two engagements between Ward and the enemy:
in the first of which, on the 10th, opposed to two
hundred Mexicans, he was victorious, having killed
twenty-five of their number ; in the next, opposed to
sixteen hundred, he sustained an unequal contest for a
whole day, and then made good his retreat towards
Victoria, agreeably to the orders of Fannin. He was
subsequently overtaken by the enemy, and forced to surrender.

Thus was the force of Col. Fannin, which had not
been above five hundred, divided, when about six hundred of the enemy came in sight of Goliad on the 17th.

On the appearance of this force, Col. Horton was
immediately despatched with a small detachment, to
reconnoitre. A skirmish took place, in which Horton
sustained himself in a gallant manner against very unequal numbers. Seeing that Horton was hard pressed,
Dr. Shackleford, with the permission of Col. Fannin, led
out his gallant little company, the " Red Rovers," from
Alabama ; who, in their eagerness for a fight, rushed
into the river, the San Antonio—the enemy being on the
opposite side—without regard to the convenience of a

ferry close at hand, and pushed on to sustain Horton. In the mean time, a cannon having been discharged from the fort, the enemy retreated, when the volunteers all returned, and regained the fort, without loss, about night-fall.

It was now a critical moment with the little garrison. They had every reason to expect the appearance of the enemy again next day, reinforced; and it appeared that they must either abandon the fort or stand a siege, for which they were not prepared. Col. Fannin was urged by some to abandon the fort immediately, taking advantage of the night to retreat; others opposed, on the ground, that their chief reliance was upon their superiority in the use of fire-arms, which, in case of an attack at night, could avail them little. Fannin said he had only waited to be reinforced by Major Ward and Captain King. "As I have given them a reasonable time to come up, and as my situation is becoming more critical every hour, I have determined to abandon my position at break of day to-morrow. I have kept my scouts in the saddle since I heard of the capture of the Alamo, searching for oxen to convey away my cannon and spying for the enemy. They met with parties of them yesterday, and exchanged a few shots. They could not discover their strength; and I have concluded, that it is the enemy's advanced guard. If so, I have no longer time for delay."—It was suggested to Fannin that he should abandon his cannon, on account of the necessary delay of removing them by oxen. "No; my cannon must go with me; I expect a fight, and I cannot do without them."

Early next morning, Col. Fannin hastened prepara-

tions for the departure of his troops. As soon as his
scouts, which had been out some time to reconnoitre,
returned, the retreat commenced. The advanced guard,
consisting of twenty-eight mounted men, were drawn
up under their commander, Capt. Horton, who, as ordered, immediately proceeded to cross the river San
Antonio at the ford, and to keep a strict look-out for the
enemy. The Infantry next marched out of the fort,
and proceeded noiselessly down to the river. There,
owing to the rapidity of the stream, and its steep and
miry banks, they were a long time delayed in crossing
their cannon and extra arms. This effected, they proceeded on their retreat nine miles, when Fannin was
compelled either to desert his cannon or rest his oxen.
The latter he determined on. The guard, which were
some distance in advance, upon perceiving the main
body halt, stopped by the road-side and kindled a fire,
for it was piercing cold. They had seated themselves
but a few minutes when they heard a rumbling noise.
Capt. Horton sprung up and listened attentively.
Again a hoarse, rumbling noise along the prairie. It
was, it was the cannon's deafening roar. Capt. Horton and his men leaped into their saddles, and dashed
in the direction of the main body under Fannin ; when,
what was their amazement to behold an immense body
of the enemy's cavalry, directly between them and their
companions, and still more pouring out of a hollow
upon the upper side of the road. The enemy were
nineteen hundred strong, under the command of Urrea.
There were, among them, the Tampico and a part of
the Morellos' battalion, the finest troops in Mexico, dis-
ciplined in the best manner by foreign generals, and

maintaining a high character for bravery. They prepared for the assault ; they charged ; the cannon roared, and as the circling smoke arose, Horton and his men saw the enemy fall back, and with them full many a horse without his rider. They charged again and again with like success. Capt. Horton and his men were discovered, and compelled to retreat. Fannin and his men—prepared to make another Thermopylæ in Texas—to fight, as had their companions at the Alamo, till not a man should be left to tell their fate—sustained themselves with the most heroic resolution. Fannin was wounded, but still was ever where his presence was most needed, continually, by his example, encouraging his men. The contest was continued from two o'clock, when it began, until night closed upon the scene. Though the Texan rifles told fatally on their ranks, the Mexican soldiers fought with determined valor. The Tampico battalion was nearly cut to pieces. From five to seven hundred Mexicans fell during the fight. Of the Texans, seven were killed, and about sixty badly wounded.

Fannin would have retreated during the night, but he could not remove his brave companions who were wounded, and he would not abandon them to a ruthless enemy. He therefore entrenched himself in the best manner he could. In the morning, the enemy having been reinforced by artillery, fired a few cannon shots, and then a flag of truce appeared from their camp. Directly their united force was drawn up in an imposing manner, and marched along in view of the Texans. The flag was sent into the Texan camp, and received. The little Texan band was exhausted, having been hard

9

at work most of the night fortifying themselves, with scarce any provisions and little water.   If they renew-ed the fight, their ammunition would soon fail, when they would inevitably be butchered.   Col. Fannin, seeing fur-ther resistance vain, and wishing to save the lives of his men, met Gen. Urrea between the two armies.   A treaty was drawn up and *signed* by both the Mexican and Texan officers.   The treaty stipulated that Fannin and his men should be treated as prisoners of war, marched back to Goliad, and detained nine days; at the expiration of which time, all the volunteers from the United States were to be shipped to New Orleans at the expense of the Mexican Government.   Fannin, and the citizens of Texas under his command, were to continue prisoners of war, until they were exchanged, or the war conclu-ded.   The Texans delivered up their arms, and were marched to Goliad, where they were left with a small guard.   In the course of a few days, they suspected, from the manner of their treatment, that the Mexicans did not intend to deal honorably with them.   They thought, if treachery was to be the order of the day, they could lose nothing by being in advance of their wily foe, and resolved to recapture the fort.   Their plan would have succeeded beyond a doubt, had they not communicated it to Fannin, who opposed its execution, saying, that hav-ing signed a treaty, so long as he did not positively know that the enemy intended him false, his honor compelled him to comply with its terms.   Thus was lost the last chance of life to these devoted men.   Despatches had been sent to Santa Anna, at Bexar.   That now ela-ted and haughty chief, thinking to drown rebellion in blood, and to extinguish aid in terror, ordered the execution of the prisoners at Goliad! In a council of his officers, after much debate and difference of opinion, he hastily rose, and in passion exclaimed, " *Si, si, si*"—Yes, yes, yes—(it shall be done ;) signed the death-warrant of the martyrs, put his own seal upon it, and handed it to a courier. On the morning after the arrival of the courier at Goliad, the 17th of March, Palm Sunday, the unsuspecting prisoners were marched out of the fort in the direction of the coast, as if, in fulfilment of the treaty, the volunteers from the United States were to be sent home ; but Texans, as well as volunteers, were marched out, in three divisions! and in single file! and by the side of each stalked a foe, armed with musket and bayo-net! They saw their fate. They were ordered to halt: the signal of death. They were nearly all instantly lifeless ; here and there one might be seen in the death-grapple with the foe! but it was soon over. They fell on the soil they had defended,—the vic-tims of cruelty, and the martyrs of liberty. Brave men! they fell not in vain ; their blood, like the dragon's teeth, sown upon the earth, caused armed men " to rise and rush into battle." The Indepen-dence of Texas was secured ; the humiliation of Mexico decreed. This " black day of Goliad" decreed what San Jacinto sealed. Yes, and long shall the Mexican, " guiltless of the blood of that day, feel the Anglo-American steel."

Fannin, who had been wounded, and in a separate apartment, was informed of his fate. He said, to the messenger, " Tell them I am ready." His only request was, that he should not be shot in the head. When up-on the fatal spot,—pushing aside the soldier, who, with trembling hand, was tying a handkerchief upon his head, —he righted it himself, then bared his breast, and fell.

The number of Texan prisoners, at the time of the massacre, was about four hundred ; the detachment of Ward, which had surrendered, making a part. Out of the four hundred, about six or seven men escaped.*

---

* About this time fourteen Texan prisoners were under sentence of death at Matamoras.

## CHAPTER X.

In the mean time, the Convention had adjourned, on the 18th, having, besides a Declaration of Independence, drawn up and passed a Constitution, several laws, and established an Executive Government, *ad interim*. This Government was clothed with full, ample, and plenary powers, to do all and any thing which was contemplated to be done by the General Congress of the People, under the powers granted by the Constitution.

David G. Burnett was elected President.

Lorenzo de Zavala, Vice President.

Col. Carson, Secretary of State.

Baily Hardiman, Secretary of Treasury.

Col. Thos. J. Rusk, Secretary of War.

Col. Robert Potter, Secretary of the Navy.

David Thomas, Attorney General.

J. R. Jones, Post Master General.

The army under Gen. Houston had remained on the Colorado until the 26th. It had increased to about thirteen hundred men, who were in high spirits, and anxious to meet the enemy. They were now, considering the short time which had elapsed since they took the field, and their character of raw recruits, in an admirable state of subordination.

The enemy, in the mean time, in several divisions, had

9*

advanced eastward.　　The advance of one division under Gen. Sezma, had reached the Colorado on the 22d.

On the 26th Gen. Houston, having intelligence of the approach of other forces of the enemy above and below him, and thinking his position insecure, fell back upon the Brazos.

This movement,—which has been the theme of much discussion, has excited a good deal of angry feeling, and for which Gen. Houston has been much blamed,— demands a few remarks.　The writer, though possessed, perhaps, of every advantage one could have for getting correct information in respect to it, was unable entirely to satisfy his own mind.　His opinion is, first, that the Texan army on the Colorado was in a critical situation ; and that, though it was in good spirits, and ready to fight the enemy, and might, and probably would, have been victorious, had an engagement took place, yet that a victory on the Colorado, under the circumstances, would not have been so signal and cheap to the Texans as under other circumstances, which might not only be supposed, but might probably, and did actually, occur at San Jacinto ; and, secondly, that, for the retreat from the Colorado—and, by anticipation, he will say, from the Brazos subsequently—there were reasons known only to the Commander-in-Chief and a *few* confidential officers, which have not yet, and probably will not be soon, fully disclosed.*　He will only state, in addition—as matter for the curious—not his own, but the opinion of some, he believes many, in

---

* One of these reasons was undoubtedly the expectation of artillery, of which there was yet not a single piece in the army.

Texas, and even some officers of the army, that there was some understanding between the officer then in command of the United States forces on the Texan frontier and Gen. Houston, which influenced the movements of the latter.

On the 27th, Gen. Houston, with the main body of the Texan army, reached the Brazos at San Felippe, from whence, for the sake of a secure position, he proceeded some distance above, to Grosse's Retreat, leaving a force of about two hundred men under Capt. Baker to guard San Felippe, and sending another small detachment farther down, to Old Fort, to guard the crossing there.   At Grosse's, Gen. Houston availed himself of a steamboat, with which to move his troops suddenly to any point they should be needed.

On the 29th, there was a false alarm of the approach of the enemy on San Felippe, whereupon the inhabitants hastily moved their goods across the Brazos, and set fire to the town.

Early on the morning of the 10th of April, the advance of the enemy's cavalry appeared at San Felippe, and soon after the main body.   Gen. Houston kept a most vigilant eye on their movements.   They were prevented from crossing the river at San Felippe by the high water, as well as by the force opposed by Capt. Baker.

On the 11th, it was ascertained that a division of the enemy had began to cross the river at Old Fort, and that another division had reached Brazoria by way of the coast; whereupon Gen. Houston made preparations to cross his troops over the river, which was effected on the 12th.

From the Brazos, Gen. Houston took the line of march eastward, to "Donahue's," at which place roads, running in the direction of Nacogdoches and Buffalo Bayou, intersect. Having previously, from the Brazos, sent despatches East, to the Red Lands—threatening to carry the war to their doors if they did not turn out—and also orders to volunteers from the United States, then advancing to join him, to halt and fortify on the Trinity, Gen. Houston, on leaving Donahue's, was about to take the road in the direction of Nacogdoches, but circumstances fortunately directed his march towards Harrisburgh.

The division of the enemy, which had now crossed the Brazos, was commanded by Santa Anna in person, who, not knowing the force and position of Gen. Houston, seems to have thought that the war was over, and that Texas was won; he, therefore, hastily proceeded to take possession of the small towns of Harrisburgh and New Washington, which places he caused to be burned on the 17th and 20th. But he was mistaken—and never was man more awfully mistaken; the Texans were close upon him; on the 18th they arrived opposite Harrisburgh. During the day, very opportunely for the Texans, and unfortunately for the enemy, a Mexican courier was taken by that most able Texan spy and brave soldier, Deaf Smith. By this courier Gen. Houston got possession of despatches and documents showing the situation, numbers, plans, and movements of the enemy. On the morning of the 19th, the Texan army crossed and proceeded down the right bank of Buffalo Bayou, to within about a half mile of its junction with the San Jacinto. Here, on the morning of the 20th, they took up a position in the edge of timber skirting the Bayou, having the timber in the rear, and in front an extensive prairie, interspersed with a few islands of timber.

Fortunately for the Texans, they had now received two pieces of artillery,* and, more fortunate still, were about to meet with but one division of Santa Anna's army, and that commanded by himself in person : having thus the chance of striking a decisive blow, with comparatively little risk.

They had occupied their position but a short time, when Santa Anna came marching up in front, with his army in battle array. He was repulsed by a discharge from the Texan artillery, whereupon he fell back, and with his infantry occupied an island of timber about a quarter of a mile distant from the left of the Texan encampment ; a little more remote, to the right of the same, he planted his artillery ; and at an intermediate point, his cavalry.

During the day there were several skirmishes between the two armies. One of the most important, as substantially related by Gen. Houston, was between the Texan artillery and the Invincibles of Santa Anna. Just as the former had reached the summit of a swell in the prairie, the latter, in their imposing uniform of high white caps and white pantaloons, appeared dashing down an opposite swell. The Texans opened a fire of their artillery, when the Invincibles, taken by surprize, broke and retreated. In the result of this

* A timely donation from the citizens of Cincinnati, Ohio—the result, in a considerable degree, of the zeal and liberality of W. M. Corry, Esq.

affair, the Texans not only had a decided advantage over the enemy, but gained confidence. The *Invincibles* had yielded.

Another action of some importance was towards the close of the day, between about eighty men under Col. Sherman and the enemy's cavalry. This was at the distance of about three quarters of a mile from the Texan camp, near the San Jacinto, where the enemy had then taken a position in the edge of the timber skirting the river, from whence, in front of their camp, they had thrown up a considerable breastwork. Sherman went out to reconnoitre and to get possession of the enemy's artillery, supposed to be at an intermediate point between the two encampments; with the understanding that he was to be sustained by a body of infantry under Col. Willard, which was at the same time drawn out. Not finding the piece of artillery, which had been removed, Sherman proceeded to reconnoitre. Seeing the enemy's cavalry drawn up in front of their entrenchment, ready for an engagement, he charged upon them, drove them back behind their infantry, sustained the fire of the latter for some minutes, and then, in danger of being surrounded and cut off by superior numbers, after having performed some feats of daring chivalry, retreated, with the loss of advantage, though not of credit.*

During the morning, the ever memorable morning, of

---

* In this affair there seems to have been some misunderstanding of orders, or, whilst it was in progress, some change discovered in the relative position of the two armies, which resulted in the determination of Gen. Houston not to sustain Sherman, and in an order to the latter to return to camp.

the 21st, the enemy, reinforced by five hundred choice troops under Gen. Cos, were seen actively engaged in fortifying their position.  It was time that the great conflict for the soil of Texas should be decided ; the Texans were impatient; delay would only increase the already great disparity of the forces opposed. Gen. Houston held a council of his officers.  It was determined to attack the enemy at their breastwork. Gen. Houston relied upon the impetuosity of the Texans in a charge : he was not deceived.  He gave orders for the bridge over Sim's Bayou, on the only accessible road to the settlements on the Brazos, to be destroyed, to prevent all escape ; and at half past three o'clock P. M. the army began to move in three divisions.  The General himself lead the van.  They moved on with the stillness of death ; not a drum, nor fife, nor voice was heard.  Every one was rousing his soul for the conflict.  When within two hundred yards of the enemy, they were formed in line of battle, and received with a shower of musket balls and grape shot.  They then marched to the attack with trailed rifles—silent, but swift and determined.  When within seventy yards the word was given, "fire !"—and an instantaneous blaze poured upon the enemy the missiles of destruction, literally mowing them down into the arms of death.    Then the word " charge !" was given, accompanied by the soul-stirring tune of " Yankee Doodle." The effect was electrical ; language cannot describe its exhilarating power ; new ardor seized the souls of the Texans ; their native country, her victories and her power, came to their minds ; they felt that they were invincible.  " Yankee Doodle" was heard above the roar of arms; and, with the shout of "the Alamo," they rushed upon their foe,—and victory rewarded their valor, and vengeance atoned for their wrongs. Seven hundred Mexicans lay a sacrifice to the shades of departed heroes slaughtered at the Alamo and Goliad.

Thus ended the glorious battle of San Jacinto, and the Mexican dominion in Texas.*

\* See Appendix, No. 8.

## CHAPTER XI.

WITH the termination of the battle of San Jacinto, which sealed the Independence of Texas, the Texan Revolution might not improperly be considered as ending. But believing a continued, though brief, narrative of the more interesting events which resulted immediately upon the decisive battle of the 21st, will be both interesting and useful, the writer will proceed with that narrative down to the adjournment of the first Congress in December, 1836.

The invincible Santa Anna was now a prisoner* in the hands of the Texans. Should he be hung upon the first tree? Should he be shot? Or should his life be spared, and a treaty made with him? Policy and vengeance were opposed; and whilst the blood of slaughtered victims demanded the latter, the safety of the living, perhaps, more imperiously demanded the former. Seven thousand Mexicans were yet under arms in Texas; they might yet give battle to their foe— might more fearfully lay waste the country, and finally fortify themselves on the frontier—or they might, perhaps, at the will of their chief, lay down their arms and march out of the country. Policy prevailed in the mind of the Commander-in-Chief of the army of Texas;

* See Appendix, No. 1.

10

Santa Anna was spared, and a treaty made with him.

In the mean time, the Government *ad interim,* which had been organized at Washington on the 17th of March, for the sake of a more ready communication with foreign nations, and the supervision of naval and maritime affairs, had removed to Harrisburgh, on Buffalo Bayou; and hence, on the rapid march of the enemy upon that place, to Galveston Island, where it received the news of the battle of San Jacinto on the 25th. President Burnet arrived at the camp of Gen. Houston on the 1st of May.

In consequence of the treaty already made between Santa Anna and Houston, the former had issued orders to Generals Filisola and Gaona, then upon the Brazos, to countermarch to Bexar, and to Gen. Urrea, to fall back upon Victoria. These orders were promptly obeyed. Thus had hostilities ceased.

Whatever opinion President Burnet and the members of his Cabinet generally might have had as to the policy of the treaty entered into by Gen. Houston, no question was instituted as to his authority to make that treaty, particularly as it was made in the presence and with the sanction of Gen. Rusk, Secretary of War. The Government, therefore—considering its faith as pledged for the personal security of Santa Anna—as the first and most important measure demanding its action, turned its attention to provide for the evacuation of Texas by the Mexican troops. For this purpose it entered into a second treaty with Santa Anna; in which it was stipulated by the latter, that he would not again take up arms, nor use his influence to cause them to be taken up, against Texas, during the existing war; that the Mexican troops should immediately march beyond the Rio Grande; that all property captured, in their possession, should be given up, and none taken without the consent of the owners; and that all Texan prisoners should be immediately released. By the former it was stipulated, that for the Texan prisoners released, an equal number of Mexicans should be exchanged. There were other conditions of the treaty not immediately to be made known. This treaty—which was soon ratified at Velasco, to which place President Burnet removed with his Cabinet—so soon as the conditions of it now specified were published, met with very great and general opposition in Texas, on the ground, first, that Santa Anna deserved death; and, secondly, that no reliance could be placed upon the fulfilment of the treaty on his part. And when, on the 1st of June, another important part of the treaty was about to be executed in the release of Santa Anna, the popular excitement became very great. Santa Anna, however, had embarked on board the schooner Invincible for Vera Cruz. Two Commissioners, Zavala and Hardiman, had been appointed to accompany him, from whose high character and talents the most important results were expected. But just as the Commissioners were about to embark, on the morning of the 3d, a company of volunteers arrived from New Orleans. They were much excited against Santa Anna, and strongly opposed to his release. This opposition, together with that of the people of the surrounding country, induced the Executive, on the morning of the 4th, to order the debarkation of Santa Anna.

Thus undoubtedly was lost much, if not all, the good which could ever result to Texas from sending Santa Anna home to Mexico. Had he arrived in Mexico *at the time.* and under the *circumstances,* contemplated by the Government, the result might, and not very unlikely would, have been the recognition of the Independence of Texas by Mexico.

Immediately as the Government had recovered itself from the embarrassment now described, it was precipitated into another, which arose in the army. The soldiers having suffered much for want of supplies, and thinking, whether truly or not, that the Government had it in its power to relieve them, but neglected to do so, had become much and generally excited, when intelligence reached them that Santa Anna was about to be liberated. This added fuel to the flame ; indignation was depicted upon every countenance ; and abuse, in no measured terms, was lavished upon the President and his Cabinet.

The result was, that an officer was despatched to the Seat of Government, with resolutions requiring that various specified measures should be acted upon immediately. This officer, on his arrival at Velasco, not being received in the manner he thought himself entitled to be, attempted the arrest of the President, not doubting, considering the great and general dissatisfaction with the Government, which existed as well on the part of citizens as soldiers, that he would be sustained. But, no : much to the credit of the citizens, they would not allow mob-law, and resolved that the Government, right or wrong, should be supported.

On the 9th, the celebrated Protests of Santa Anna were laid before President Burnet and his Cabinet.

Santa Anna protested—1st. Against the treatment he had received, as not comporting with his dignity as the head of a respectable nation. 2d. Against the treatment, as prisoner, and ill usage of Gen. Woll, who had entered the Texan camp with a flag of truce. 3d. Against the non-fulfilment of the stipulated exchange of prisoners on the part of the Government of Texas, though all the Texan prisoners had been liberated in the army under his command. 4th. He protested that the most essential part of the treaty, stipulating his own release and passage home to Vera Cruz, had not been fulfilled. 5th. Against the violence committed on his person, and the abuse to which he had been exposed in his debarkation at Velasco. Finally, he protested against the violence shown him in his continued and close imprisonment, surrounded by sentinels, and suffering insupportable privations.

These Protests were replied to by President Burnet, as follows :—

"As to your first protest, I do not precisely understand the kind of treatment objected to. If your Excellency alludes to your accommodations, I would reply that I have subjected my own sick family to hardships on your account; that we are destitute of comforts, is mainly attributable to your Excellency's visit to our country; and hence we feel less regret that you should feel our privations.

" The cause of your *second* protest, I do sincerely deplore; but the Government is not responsible for it. Our orders were contravened by the Commander-in-

10*

Chief.   We understand that the conduct of Gen. Woll was not with conspicuous discretion.*

"In respect to your *third* protest, your Excellency is mistaken.   I have no official information of a single Texan prisoner having been released under the treaty.

"In reply to your *fourth* protest, we would say, that late events have given us much pain.   You are, however, mistaken in your assertion, that we were aware that you had punctually fulfilled all your engagements. On the contrary, we have been informed that many cattle and some slaves were taken away by the retreating army.   Besides, it has been reported that the walls of the Alamo were prostrated, and the artillery there melted.   This wanton dilapidation and destruction is the more odious because of peculiar reminiscences connected with the Alamo.

"In reply to your *fifth* protest, I have to state, what you know, that your debarkation was a compulsory measure.

"To your *final* protest, I reply, that, while you are a prisoner, ordinary precautions are inevitable.   I have not been apprised of any thing more ; and your privations (as said) are those we suffer ourselves."

---

* What the orders of President Burnet were, which were contravened, is not known.   But it is known that Gen. Woll, having behaved himself very imprudently in the Texan camp, was put under guard, more for his own safety than any thing else.

## CHAPTER XII.

IN the mean time, the Mexican army, under Filisola, had evacuated Texas. A division of the Texan army, under Gen. Rusk, had advanced to Goliad, to see that the conditions of the treaty stipulated by Santa Anna were observed.

The sympathy for the people of Texas on the part of the citizens of the United States, which had been so conspicuously shown in the previous autumn and win- ter, had not diminished. It had doubtless, in a con- siderable degree, been sustained by the presence of the highly respectable Texan Commissioners, who exerted themselves in various places in the United States to enlighten the minds of their countrymen upon the causes and merits of the struggle in progress in Texas.

In March, a company of volunteers had arrived from New York. Another company from Cincinnati, Ohio, had arrived under the command of Col. Sherman, just in time to bear a conspicuous part in the struggle at San Jacinto. Mississippi had poured forth her chiv- alry; from whence two hundred men under Gen. F. Huston, and forty under Col. Quitman, were on the march, and in Texas, before the battle of San Ja- cinto. Another company of four hundred and fifty men arrived soon after, as stated, at Velasco, under Gen. T. J. Green.

In the city of New York, a splendid entertainment

was given by the friends of Texas, which was hon-
ored by the presence of Generals Ripley, and Hamilton, by Preston, Peyton, and other distinguished
guests. Philadelphia also shared the enthusiasm
of its sister cities, and sent out a company of volunteers. Indeed, almost from Maine to Georgia,
men acquainted with the character of the struggle
in progress in Texas, began to feel that such a
crisis had there arrived, that a regard to national
obligations of neutrality, in respect of that struggle,
could have no place; when, in the language of the
distinguished Senator of Missouri, "in fact, a man
should have no head to think; nothing but a heart to
feel, and an arm to strike."

The Government itself, of the United States, did not
look upon the Texan war with indifference: it sent
an army upon the Texan frontier, to keep in check the
savages of the North. This, even had it intended no
countenance whatever to the struggling Texans, it was
bound to do in sheer justice, and not to allow the savages it had sent West to break in upon and destroy the
defenceless; as a large part of the people of Texas were
at the time.

Even in Legislative halls, the voices of those illus-
trious in the councils of their country, were raised in
favor of Texas. Mr. Benton, in the Senate of the
United States, in a speech already quoted, sustained
the cause of Texas in a very able and eloquent manner. Mr. Clay, also, from a Committee of the same
body on Foreign Relations, on the 18th of June, reported favorably to the recognition of the Independence
of Texas, so soon as it should appear that she had in

" successful operation, a Civil Government capable of performing the duties and fulfilling the obligations of an Independent Power." On which occasion the distinguished Senator made in connection the following remarks :

" If the contest has been unequal, it has, nevertheless, been maintained by Texas with uncommon resolution, undaunted valor, and eminent success. And the recent signal and splendid victory—in which that portion of the Mexican army which was commanded by Gen. Santa Anna, the President of the Mexican Government, in person, was entirely overthrown with unexampled slaughter, compared with the inconsiderable loss on the other side, put to flight and captured, including among the prisoners the President himself and staff— may be considered as decisive of the Independence of Texas."

On the 27th, a resolution was offered by Mr. Preston, for sending an agent or commissioner to Texas, which was adopted. In the Legislature of South Carolina, also, the cause of Texas was nobly sustained by Poinsett, by Hamilton, and others.

In the mean time, the disastrous campaign under Santa Anna had caused great excitement in Mexico ; and it was resolved by the Government to make a mighty effort to retrieve the advantage lost, and to restore the credit of their arms. Accordingly, early in the summer, preparations were made on an extensive scale for another invasion of Texas ; six thousand troops had been concentrated at Matamoras ; a forced loan of two millions of dollars was authorized ; the port of Matamoras declared open for the importation of provisions from the interior duty free, and from abroad duty paid *in kind;* and exertions were made to gain Indian alliances.

As soon as intelligence of these hostile movements reached Texas, active and zealous preparations were made to meet the storm. Between four and five thousand men were soon under arms; whole villages were left without a single man; the citizens of the Colorado, not again disposed to leave the banks of their beautiful river, except to march *Westward,* were particularly prompt in turning out in obedience to the call of the Secretary of War. Bounty lands were offered by the Government to volunteers, as follows: to those who should serve six months, six hundred and forty acres; to those who should serve during the war, twelve hundred and eighty; and to those who should serve three months, three hundred and twenty. These lands were made the property of the lawful heirs of those to whom they were granted, in case of the death of the grantee.

Difficulties in the interior of Mexico soon made it necessary to employ her forces and resources in another direction, and the proposed invasion of Texas was abandoned.

During the summer of the year 1836, the disposal of Santa Anna was a constant theme of excitement in Texas. In the month of August, a plot for his release was discovered at Columbia, where he then was. A vessel, the "Passaic," Capt. Hughes, arrived from New Orleans at Brazoria, where she discharged a part of her cargo, and proceeded to Columbia. There, one Peges, a Spaniard, to whom the cargo had been consigned, and who was in part owner of it, carried to the tent of Santa Anna a bottle, represented to contain bitters, but really containing opium, designed to be administered to the guard, that, by its operation, the captive chief might make his escape.

Suspicions were excited and inquiries made, when a principal in the plot came forward and gave information. It appeared, by a written document, that the Mexican consul at New Orleans, was a partner in the plot. The result was that the vessel was seized, Peges and a sailor put in irons, as also Santa Anna and Almonte. At this time Santa Anna endeavored to destroy himself, by swallowing opium ; which produced only nausea.

The final disposal of Santa Anna was reserved to the Constitutional Government about to be established.

## CHAPTER XIII.

The period was now approaching for the people of Texas to go into a Constitutional Election of a President, Vice-President, and Members of Congress. President Burnet had issued his Proclamation, ordering that election, and requiring that, at the same time, there should be an expression of the public sentiment in respect to the annexation of Texas to the United States.

Gen. Austin was nominated to the Presidency on the 9th of August.

Gen. Houston—who had been for some time absent in the United States for the purpose of medical aid in recovering from a wound received at the battle of San Jacinto—had again appeared in Texas, and was nominated to the Presidency at Columbia, on the 20th, by more than six hundred persons.

Early in the month of September, Samuel Houston, the " hero of San Jacinto," was elected first President of the Republic of Texas, and Mirabeau B. Lamar first Vice-President.

In respect to the annexation of Texas to the United States, the People, " with a unanimity unparalleled, declared that they would be united to the great political family of the North."

The first Congress of the People met at Columbia on the 3d of October. Never, perhaps, had a Congress more to do, and less to do with. It had to bring order and system out of chaos, and raise means where none existed. The country was in a very disorganized state ; the people impoverished ; and the treasury exhausted. There was a large amount of claims and demands upon the Government ; there was no law nor judiciary ; and the army was naked and starving.

It is not the purpose of the writer to give a history of the various deliberations and acts of the Congress, by which it met the wants of the country, in its domestic as well as foreign relations, but only to notice some of the more important. During the session were passed, among others, the following acts :

An act authorising the President to fill vacancies in the offices of Treasurer, Secretary of State, Secretary of the Treasury, &c.

An act for the relief of Erastus Smith, allowing him, in consideration of his sacrifices, and very valuable services in the cause of Texas, the privilege of selecting any forfeited house and lot in San Antonio which he might choose, and to hold the same, himself and heirs, in fee simple forever ; and to take possession of such house and lot so soon as the forfeiture of the same should be ascertained in a legal way. Also, allowing him to locate any where in the public domain one league and labore of land, and to hold the same, as the aforesaid house and lot.

An act authorizing the President to appoint a Minister, with ample and plenary powers, to proceed to the United States, to negociate for the recognition of the Independence of Texas, and for the speedy annexation of the same to the United States, according to the expressed wish of the people of Texas.

11

An act authorizing the President to issue *bonds* of one thousand dollars each, to an amount not exceeding five million dollars, to bear interest to the purchaser not exceeding ten per cent., to be redeemed at the expiration of thirty years; and to be signed by the President and Secretary of State, and countersigned by the Secretary of the Treasury; and to be offered for sale by two Commissioners, to be appointed by the President, in the United States, or in England; said Commissioners to be required, from time to time, to report to the Secretary of the Treasury the amount of bonds sold, and expenses attending the sale of the same.    The act provided also, that at each meeting of Congress an account should be presented by the Secretary of the Treasury of the sales made of the bonds, and of the appropriation of the proceeds; that the Commissioners, however, might sell bonds to the amount of two millions, redeemable in less time than thirty, but not less than five years; that the holders of the bonds should have the privilege of purchasing, at the minimum Government price, the lands of the Government, and of paying for the same in these bonds; that, finally, for the paying the interest on the bonds and their final redemption, the public faith should be pledged, as also the proceeds of the sale of the public domain, and the taxes on land after 1838.

An act incorporating a Rail-road, Navigation and Banking Company.

An act for the increase of the Navy,* providing for

* The history of the naval affairs of Texas, with very little exception, does not come within the scope of the author's work.

the purchase and fitting out of a sloop of war and two armed steam vessels.

In addition to those on which were passed the acts now specified, Congress had in deliberation other important subjects; of which one was the authorizing foreigners to hold land in Texas. On the questions— First, Is it expedient to allow foreign volunteers the privilege of selling their lands to aliens? Secondly, Is it expedient to allow those aliens, who have aided Texas, the privilege of holding land in the Republic?—Mr. Baker reported, first, that, in favor of those who had left their country, their homes of peace and plenty, many of whom had been sacrificed by a ruthless foe whilst fighting for the rights and liberty of Texas, and all of whom had suffered much, Government was in justice bound to provide every advantage in its power; and secondly, that not to allow those—who had advanced money and forwarded supplies to Texas in her darkest hour, when a large part of her own citizens had abandoned her—to hold lands in Texas, would be ingratitude, besides that it would be depriving many such of lands which they had already purchased, and to which they were justly entitled.

Another subject of great interest which the Congress had in discussion, was the disposal of Santa Anna. It seems to have been the desire of the President to send him to the city of Washington, with the view of his entering into some treaty with the Government of the United States. This was opposed on the ground, first, that Santa Anna had not fulfilled his part of the treaty which had been made, or that Filisola had not, which must, under the circumstances, be considered the same thing: that, secondly, no reliance could be placed upon the promises of Santa Anna, as had been evinced by his conduct in Mexico, having been at one time of the Federal party, and solemnly sworn, in the face of the world and high Heaven, to support the Constitution of 1824—and then of the Central party, employing military force against the very individuals who had assisted him in his first professions; and who had, moreover, witnessed the slaughter at the Alamo, and had authorized the massacre of Fannin: that, thirdly, he could not treat with the Government at Washington, for that the Executive of the United States had been formally notified by the Government of Mexico, that none of the acts of Santa Anna would be recognized by that Government : that, fourthly, Santa Anna might be made most useful to Texas by being retained a prisoner, for that undoubtedly he yet had powerful friends in Mexico, who, well aware that were another army sent into Texas, he would be sacrificed, that event would be less likely to happen ; and that, in case Texas should invade Mexico, as was contemplated, the name and person of Santa Anna with the invading army might be turned to good account.

On the contrary, it was maintained, in favor of the release of Santa Anna, first, that he was a dead expense to the Government: secondly, that the proposed proclamation in Santa Anna's name at the head of an invading army was a wild scheme : and, thirdly, that advantage might accrue from his being set at liberty, for that he would endeavor to get into power again in Mexico, in which, succeeding, he might acknowledge the Independence of Texas,—and not succeeding, he would foment civil commotion, and thus grant Texas a respite ; but, on the worst supposition, should he, after again getting into power, again attempt the subjugation of Texas, he would receive the execrations of the civilized world, and Texas would be justified, and her cause sustained.*

Soon after, a resolution passed the Senate authorising the President to liberate, at his discretion, the Mexican officers and prisoners, with the *exception* of Generals Santa Anna and Almonte. This resolution was sent to the President for his signature, and returned with his veto ; upon which there arose an animated debate. Mr. Everett declared the question before the Senate to be—Shall Santa Anna be released by the President *without* the concurrence of the Senate ? He argued the constitutionality of the resolution, and the inexpediency of the immediate release of Santa Anna, according to the known wish of the Executive ; he remarked upon the insufficiency of the reasons advanced by the Executive for the release of Santa Anna, and the sending him to Washington City, as was proposed. These reasons, as stated by the Senator, were, first, the insalubrity of the climate of the Brazos, and the probable improvement of the health of the distinguished captive by a removal to Washington ; secondly, the *diet* of the captive, which was not what he was accustomed to, and which might prove highly injurious, or even fatal to him ; thirdly, reasons founded

* The writer would here have introduced an able argument of Gen. Lamar, upon the subject of the release of Santa Anna, were it not for its great length, and his unwillingness to divide it.

11*

on policy, relating to the probable result of treaties which Santa Anna might make with the Government of Texas, or with that of the United States. Mr. Everett closed with an able philippic upon the character of Santa Anna.

The final release of Santa Anna was an Executive act. It was in the month of December. He was sent on to Washington City.

Congress allotted to the President and Cabinet salaries as follows:—To the President, $10,000; Vice-President, $3000; Secretaries of Treasury, War, Navy, &c., $3000; Postmaster-General, $2000.

Towards the last of December Congress adjourned. During its session of not quite three months, a Cabinet of character and ability had been appointed; superior, district, and county courts established; the army had been organized, clothed, and fed; and the people had been put in full possession of their civil and political rights.

# GEOGRAPHY,

## TOPOGRAPHY, STATISTICS, &c.

OF

# TEXAS.

# TO THE READER.

THE Author at first designed to have published a general description of the Soil, Climate, Scenery, Rivers, important Towns, &c. of Texas, in a connected narrative ; but, upon the suggestion of friends and others interested in the country, that a more particular account of its Geography, Topography, and Statistics, was most wanted, and would be more valuable, he adopted the plan suggested ; and the more willingly, because he had on hand ample material. This material he has obtained in different ways, and has made such use of it as would best contribute to the great object he has had in view in the composition of his work—that of rendering it the medium of the most correct and valuable information concerning Texas.

# GEOGRAPHY, &c. OF TEXAS.

## GENERAL FEATURES.

TEXAS contains 400,000 or 500,000 square miles; is larger than the kingdoms of France and Spain; has a sky as bright and a climate as mild as the south of Italy, and an atmosphere generally as pure and elastic as that of the "mountains of Circassia;" it is unsurpassed in mineral wealth, not excepting the precious metals; its soil rivals in fertility the delta of Egypt, equally adapted to the culture of two of the richest staples known to the commercial world,—sugar and cotton. It embraces within its more generally known limits—on a line running from the 32d degree North latitude, on the East, to the cross timbers on the West, a distance of four hundred miles, and from this line to the sea, a distance of one hundred miles—35,000 or 40,000 square miles, or 25,000,000 of acres, of which five or six millions will yield a bale of cotton to the acre at least, and much of it two bales, or more. At the lowest rate, then, the product will be 5,000,000 bales a year, which, at forty dollars per bale, will amount to the enormous sum of $200,000,000! Then there would be left 20,000,000 of acres for other agricultural purposes.

## LARGER DIVISIONS.

Texas may be divided into three parts, diverse in surface, soil, and somewhat in climate. First, the low alluvial country, extending from the Sabine to the Rio Grande, and from the sea, about, on an average, seventy miles interior. Secondly, the beautifully undulating country, extending from Red River and the Sabine to the neighborhood of the Rio del Norte, and from about seventy miles interior to the mountains. Thirdly, the table lands beyond the mountains.

In the first of these divisions, it is believed, is as large a portion of rich soil as can be found within the same limits on any other part of the American continent. It is almost entirely alluvial, and, with the exception of a small portion between the Sabine and the San Jacinto, of the richest kind. This division is generally free from marshes; intersected by numerous rivers; is contiguous to the sea; and for purposes of agriculture, particularly in the growth of sugar and cotton, offers more inducements to the planter than any other portion of low alluvial country within the same, or nearly the same, latitudes. The writer cannot describe the emotions with which he has looked upon some of these alluvial bottoms. The natural grandeur and beauty of the scene, together with its prospective wealth and dense population, has been to him a theme of admiring contemplation. But, as in all low countries, so there are in this, peculiar evils connected with a residence. These evils will decrease with the progressive settlement of the country : nevertheless, they will, in some degree, continue. Besides the comparative insalubrity of this region—though the resident here is fanned six months of the year by a sea breeze—it is, during the wet season, very muddy, and travelling extremely difficult ; water in it is not good ; and it teems with noisome insects, especially flies and mosquitos.

In the second division are the high, rolling, verdant prairies, the narrow wooded bottoms, the beautiful islands of timber, the quick running streams, the cool refreshing springs, and the healthful clime of Texas. Here are no noisome insects, no marshes, and no mud to annoy the traveller. Here the soil, little broken, is not inferior in quality to that of the alluvial country below ; is more easily worked ; the product as great, and more varied ; and though not so convenient to a foreign market, will have a market at home ; for here is to be the most densely populated part of Texas, if not of America ; here emigrants are pouring in with almost unexampled rapidity ; and here is to be undoubtedly, to some extent, as well a manufacturing as an agricultural community. In this region the planter may raise all the cotton he can pick, all the corn he wants, and stock to almost any extent, without labor, and almost without attention.

The table lands are yet the home of the Indian, and the range of the buffalo. Little is known of them ; but they are represented by travellers to rival the table lands of Mexico ; to be, in point of soil, little inferior to the region just described ; to have even a superior climate; to be clothed in constant verdure, beautifully variegated in surface, and watered with streams as clear as crystal; to be, in fine, a Paradise.

Of the most northern portion of Texas, extending to the 42d degree of north latitude, parallel with Massachusetts and Connecticut, still less is known than of the table lands. This region is said to be intersected by many streams of water power, and to be rich in the precious metals.

## PRINCIPAL RIVERS, AND ADJACENT COUNTRY.

*Red River* may be considered as in part belonging to Texas. The vast region west of the mountains, in which it rises, and through which it rolls its majestic waters, has been yet scarce explored; but it is known to be of great fertility and of surpassing beauty. In this region will the Texan emigrant soon plant his cottage, and soon will his cotton, and his corn, and his wheat, be borne along the current of Red River to the great mart of the West.

*The Sabine* is to Texas a valuable river. It is navigable for steamboats at all seasons seventy or eighty miles, and at high water one hundred or more. Its banks are seldom overflowed, are well timbered, and generally fertile.

*The Trinity* is generally about eighty yards wide, and eight or ten feet deep, with a rapid current. At its mouth there is a broad sand bar, which is the only obstruction to its navigation by steamboats for a distance of two hundred, and, it is even said, nigh three hundred miles, to its forks. Indeed, according to very late advices from Texas, a steamboat has passed four hundred miles up this river. Its banks in many places are low, and liable to inundation. The soil, though generally good, and much of it of the first quality, is in some places rather heavy and difficult to work, though strong and productive ; in other places, light and sandy, yet capable of producing very good crops of cotton. The country on this river has an advantage in its contiguity to the United States, and an outlet for its products into Galveston Bay.

*The Brazos,* with the exception of the bar at its mouth, is navigable at all seasons for steamboats of the largest class for about fifty or sixty miles ; at high water, for a much greater distance ; and it is confidently believed that its bed may be so improved as to admit of the passage of small boats, at most seasons, even as high as Nashville. The soil upon this river, with scarce an exception, is of the richest kind, generally of a dark brown, or chocolate color, and very deep : lower down, it is well adapted to sugar, and in every part to cotton. Its product in these staples is destined to be immense. Upon its banks the live oak is found in great abundance ; which, in many places, throws out upon the river its ponderous arms, with numerous branches, as if, lord of the soil, it would hold divided empire with the water.

On this river are the oldest American towns in Texas, the largest and most wealthy planters, and the greatest amount of business is done.

*The Colorado,* with the exception of a raft at its

mouth, which is soon to be cleared out, is believed to be navigable at most seasons, for small steamboats, as high as Bastrop, more than one hundred miles. This is, perhaps, the finest river in Texas. It is a rapid stream of clear wholesome water, about two hundred and fifty yards wide, and ten or fifteen feet deep, flowing over a pebbly bottom. Its outlet is into a beautiful expansive bay; its banks, for fifty or sixty miles from its mouth, are low, but little liable to inundation; higher up, they are bold, and in some places lofty and precipitous. There is upon this river an abundance of valuable timber; and the soil, though not so uniformly rich as that of the Brazos, is generally highly fertile, and in many places not surpassed by any in Texas.

Upon this river, which runs very nearly through the centre of Texas, it is highly probable the Seat of Government will eventually be located. Several towns have been lately laid off, and emigrants are establishing themselves in great numbers.

*The Guadaloupe*, though a principal river of Texas, is scarcely, if at all, navigable, owing to its very rapid current and short bends. It is generally about one hundred and fifty yards wide. Its waters are limpid and pure; its banks well timbered. The soil upon this river is, perhaps, surpassed by none in Texas, except that of the Brazos and Caney. The scenery is highly picturesque and beautiful, and the traveller feels, as he approaches it from the East, that he is about to enter a country of new and more interesting features.

*The San Antonia* is formed from four springs, which

rise from a small eminence four or five miles above Bexar, and, uniting their waters about a mile above that city, form a river fifty yards wide and four or five feet deep. This stream is very rapid. It flows over a pebbly bed, and its waters arc remarkably pure and wholesome. Such is their transparency, that small fish may be distinctly seen at a depth of ten feet. A little below Bexar it unites with the Medina; and though the latter is the larger branch, the two continue under the name of the San Antonio to their junction with the Guadaloupe, just before they discharge their waters into Esperitu Santo Bay.

The banks of this river are more generally high than those of any of the rivers in Eastern and Middle Texas—in many places forty or fifty feet—rocky and precipitous. The adjacent country is generally a high rolling prairie, with little timber ; its soil a dark sandy loam, exceedingly rich and productive. Its present appearance evinces a high state of improvement, and a numerous population at some former period. Numerous canals, the object of which was to irrigate the soil ; a small, and evidently secondary growth of timber ; the remains of several churches, called Missions, connected with other large buildings, are evidence of a once flourishing country.

*The Rio Grande* hardly deserves the name it bears, as, when compared with the principal rivers of America, it cannot be considered a *great* river. The portion of it forming the western boundary of this country, is generally only about two hundred yards wide, and so shallow, in many places, that vessels drawing five or six feet of water cannot ascend more than about a hundred miles, in ordinary stages of the stream. Its current is exceedingly rapid. It is navigable at all seasons for steamboats drawing three or four feet of water as far as Camargo, about two hundred miles from its mouth. In the summer of 1829, Captain Austin ascended it in a small steamboat nearly to Revilla, about three hundred miles from its mouth. He found the navigation above Camargo exceedingly difficult and dangerous. In many instances the rapidity of the current completely overpowered the action of the steam engine, and he was compelled to use tow-lines in order to make any progress. The bed of this river below Revilla is chiefly quicksand, which is constantly swept from place to place by the current, forming innumerable changing sand bars. Its banks are generally quite steep. They are often undermined in such manner during the annual freshets, that whole acres are at times suddenly precipitated into the stream, and not unfrequently the river opens to itself a new channel through the country to the distance of several miles. In many places these new channels have been cut through banks thirty or forty feet high. The Rio Grande, like the Brazos, by opening abruptly into the Gulf of Mexico, constitutes a singular exception to the ordinary harmony of Nature, as mentioned by St. Pierre, who has wisely remarked that Nature has "contrived deep bays sheltered from the general currents of the ocean, that during stormy weather the rivers might discharge themselves into them in security, and that the finny legions might resort thither for refuge at all seasons." By reference to the map, however, the intelligent naturalist will readily decide that both of these rivers have been accidentally turned away from the natural outlets; and appearances near their mouth evidently indicate that the former has, at some distant period, poured its waters into the Bay of Brazos Santiago, and the latter into the West Bay of Galveston.

## SECONDARY RIVERS.

Besides the rivers now described, there are others of less importance, though navigable to a considerable extent.

*The Neches,* it is believed, will be navigable for small steamboats to the San Antonio road, more than a hundred miles. It is generally from fifty to seventy yards wide, and from ten to fifteen feet deep. It is subject to an inundation of from two to three miles on each side. The soil upon its banks is generally a very rich and deep black mould, which will produce excellent cotton, corn, or sugar.

*The San Jacinto* is navigable for small boats twenty-five or thirty miles. The banks are generally high, and little liable to inundation.

*Buffalo Bayou* is a very singular water-course, without any current, except as caused by the tides of the sea; very deep; and navigable, from its junction with the San Jacinto to its forks at Houston, for boats of any draft of water, though too *narrow* to admit those of the largest class. The soil upon its banks is generally light and sandy.

*The San Bernard* is navigable for small boats about forty miles. The soil of its banks is, in places, light and sandy, though generally highly productive.

12*

*The Caney,* a creek, is navigable for boats of a light draft of water about thirty miles. The soil on this creek is proverbially rich, producing astonishing crops of cotton, and exceedingly well adapted to the growth of sugar.

*The Navidad* and *La Baca* run nearly parallel most of their course, and unite at no great distance from Matagorda Bay, into which they discharge their waters. They are both navigable about thirty-five miles for steamboats drawing three feet of water. They flow through a gently undulating, beautiful, and healthy country. The soil of their banks is a rich black mould, very deep, and remarkably fertile, producing, in abundance, cotton, corn, potatoes, sugar-cane, wheat, rye, oats, barley, &c. The waters of these rivers are clear, cool, and wholesome.

*The Nueces,* the former boundary between Coahuila and Texas, is navigable for very small craft seventy-five or one hundred miles. It flows mostly through an open prairie country. The soil upon its banks, though much of it excellent, is not so generally fertile as that on the other rivers of Western Texas. The scenery along much of its meandering course is said to be very beautiful.

There are many other considerable streams in Texas, which are not reckoned valuable for purposes of navigation, but upon which, especially those at the West, is a great deal of very beautiful and highly fertile country. Of these, may be mentioned the Medina, the Sobolo, and the Solado, which are in Western Texas; the Navasoto, Oyster Creek, and Chocolate Bayou, in Middle Texas; the Attoyæ and Angelina Bayous, in Eastern Texas.

## PRINCIPAL TOWNS, AND ADJACENT
## COUNTRY.

*Nacogdoches* is handsomely situated on an elevated angular plain, between and just above the junction of the beautiful Bonito on the West, and the La Nina on the East. This was one of the first of the towns established in Texas by Spain, about one hundred and twenty-five years ago, and grew, under her nurturing care, to considerable importance ; but during the revolutionary war which severed Mexico from the Spanish dominion, it often suffered the ruinous consequences of a desolating warfare. It was a military post, both under the Spanish and Mexican Governments, down to 1832, when the Central Mexican troops, stationed there, were expelled by the citizens and inhabitants of the neighboring country. It is the county seat of the county of the same name, contains about five hundred inhabitants, and is rapidly improving. It is in lat. N. 31 deg. 40 min., long. W. from Washington 17 deg. 17 min.

The country about Nacogdoches is highly picturesque, and much of it very fertile, especially the Red Lands, producing excellent cotton, corn, and other products generally raised in the same latitude. North and South of Nacogdoches, however, is a good deal of light sandy soil.

The climate of this section of country is highly salubrious—that of no portion of the globe, of the same latitude and elevation, perhaps more so. The atmosphere is dry and elastic, and has a most salutary influence on constitutions which have become impaired by a long residence in the less healthy regions bordering on the Gulf of Mexico. These, and other circumstances which might be mentioned, indicate this portion of country as the future location of the "Athens of Texas."

*San Augustine,* forty-five miles East of Nacogdoches, is a town of considerable importance, and very rapidly improving. The soil of the surrounding country is much like that of the Red Lands near Nacogdoches, producing, in great abundance, cotton, corn, rye, oats, &c. There are a few sandy ridges of pine growth, and a few small prairies, the soil of which is a rich black mould. The climate of this region is salubrious, and the water abundant and good.

*Houston,* the present Capital of the Republic, situated at the head of navigation on Buffalo Bayou, is a town of great and growing importance. It has sprung up with astonishing rapidity, and is the centre of an extensive trade. There are very different opinions in respect to its permanent importance. In some respects it is well situated for trade, and in others not; on the one hand, it is on a stream communicating with Galveston Bay, and which is at all seasons navigable, and is thus easily accessible from the sea, and it is, moreover, but a short distance from the fertile lands of the Brazos. These are its advantages. But, on the other hand, it is scarcely accessible by land in the rainy season, being surrounded by low wet prairies to a considerable extent; it has not, hence, a productive country immediately around to support it; and it has been, and, owing to local causes of disease, probably will continue to be, unhealthy. These are its disadvantages.

It now contains about four hundred good buildings and twenty-five hundred inhabitants.

*Brazoria,* the county seat of a county of the same name, is situated on the West bank of the Brazos, about twenty-five miles from its mouth. It is one of the oldest American towns in Texas, and, in point of trade, a place of importance. The soil of the surrounding country, except a small tract bordering the coast, is very rich and productive, consisting of a deep black mould resting upon a substratum of red loam ; this substratum is in many places thirty or forty feet deep, and entirely free from stones. Near the coast, the soil is quite thin, resting upon a bed of sand and shells ; it, however, produces here an abundant crop of grass, affording excellent pasturage. Cotton and Indian corn are extensively cultivated, and yield abundant crops with but little labor. Almost all kinds of culinary vegetables thrive well. Horned cattle increase in a wonderful manner, and are an immense source of wealth, as they require hardly any attention, and continue pasturing in the extensive and fertile prairies and woodlands during the whole year. Here are many of the wealthiest farmers of Texas ; of whom some are from the most Northern States in the Union, and have resided here several years, enjoying excellent health, thus proving that the climate is healthy. The water of many parts of the county is not wholesome, unless boiled or filtered. This circumstance has induced many planters to collect the rain water for family use ; such families are almost invariably healthy.

*Columbia,* about twelve miles above Brazoria, is beautifully situated on the Eastern border of an extensive and romantic prairie, a mile and a half from the Brazos. The country around it is much like that about Brazoria.

*Marion* is an important landing on the right bank of the Brazos, about half a mile from Columbia. It promises to be a place of extensive trade.

*San Felippe de Austin* deserves to be particularly mentioned for what it has been. It is situated on the West bank of the Brazos, at the North-east corner of an extensive prairie, about seventy miles above Columbia. It was formerly the Capital of the Brazos jurisdiction, and contained six hundred inhabitants at the commencement of the war. On the approach of the enemy, it was burnt. The country around partakes of that uniform character which belongs to the Brazos bottoms already described.

The climate, though not as salubrious as that of many parts of Texas, is yet of so uniform a temperature, that the ordinary clothing of the New England and Middle States is commonly worn by the inhabitants here. The summer skies are remarkably serene and beautiful, occasionally diversified by towering piles of thunder clouds, careering along the water-courses and shedding down gentle refreshing showers. The heat of the days in summer is seldom oppressive, and the nights are quite cool.

*Washington,* a place of some note, as well on account of the historical reminiscences connected with it, as its present size and rapid growth, is situated on the East bank of the Brazos, about one hundred and forty or one hundred and fifty miles from its mouth. Here the Convention, which passed the Declaration of Independence, held its sessions in the spring of 1836; here the Government *ad interim* was organized, and continued, until the approach of the enemy and other circumstances caused its removal to Harrisburgh.

The country about Washington, in point of soil and climate, is very like that already described adjacent to the towns lower down the Brazos.    Washington has undoubtedly an advantage over those towns, in being central to an extensive region of country, which, if not more fertile, is destined to be more densely populated than the bottoms below.    Its present population is about four or five hundred.

*Bastrop* is pleasantly situated in an elevated and re-markably healthy prairie, on the left bank of the Col-orado, about thirty-five miles below the mountains, and one hundred from Matagorda.    Its remarkably healthy and central position will necessarily secure to it, in a few years, a rank and importance equalled by but few cities in the Republic.    It is now a frontier town; but the extensive and rich vallies of the San Saba and Colorado, above, offer so many enticing allurements to emigrants, that it must, within a very short period, be-come the centre of one of the most populous and pro-ductive sections of Texas.

The great fertility, the unrivalled scenery, the rapid-ly increasing population, the great relative advantages of the region of country about Bastrop, considered particularly in connection with the fact, that the Seat of Government* will probably be located within its

---

* By a late act of Congress, it appears that La Grange is to be the Seat of Government after 1840.

limits, demand for it a notice in some degree com-
mensurate with its importance.

The peculiar *centrality* of this region, considered as
commencing on the Colorado river, about forty miles
below Bastrop, and extending thence to and beyond
the mountains, independent of its natural advantages,
renders it the most interesting section of Texas.

From about twelve miles below the La Bahia crossing, the Colorado becomes confined to a comparatively
narrow and deep channel.   Its banks, which are a continuation to the river of the rich, black, sandy, alluvial
highlands of the surrounding country, are generally
high—on the West side, from fifty to eighty feet above
the surface of the river at its ordinary stage.   From
the same crossing to the mountains, distant about seventy miles, the average width of the river is from
eighty to one hundred and fifty yards, and its depth sufficient, during a considerable portion of the year, for
the navigation of steamboats of from three to six feet
draft of water.   At the mountains, it rushes along its
channel with great velocity and considerable fall,
causing the roar of a cataract.   Immediately under the
South-eastern base of the mountain, it receives the pure
transparent waters of a large number of remarkably
bold lime-stone fountains ; some of which are sufficiently large, and have ample fall, to propel important machinery.   These, together with the falls of the river,
offer fine facilities and an ample field for the enterprize
of Northern manufacturers and mechanics.

The country North-west of the mountains, as reported
by the few who have ventured upon it, has a generally
fertile soil, an abundance of pure water, a surface well

adapted to agricultural pursuits, and scenery of surpassing beauty. The mountain region has inexhaustible
quarries of the purest lime-stone, and an abundance of
timber.

The water of the Colorado river, coming rapidly
down from its bold mountain fountains, is generally of remarkable coolness, transparency, and purity.
After heavy rains, it rises suddenly and becomes turbid.
Its current, though generally rapid to its mouth, becomes more gentle as it descends from the mountains.

The vast chain of prairie, extending from the La Bahia crossing, on the West side of this interesting river, to
the mountains, is inferior to no part of Texas in beauty
of surface and fertility of soil. These prairies are
generally of a rich, deep, black, loose, and sandy character, easily cultivated and remarkably productive,
having an abundance of fine running water, and timber convenient. The same general character belongs
to the extensive region lying West of the Colorado, on
Buckner's creek, the Navidad, La Baca, and Guadaloupe;
on the latter of which rivers, grows, in great profusion,
the much celebrated musquit grass, affording ample
pasturage, both in summer and winter, for the most
extensive stock of the herdsman.

On the Colorado are very large bottoms, covered
throughout the winter with a rich rye pasturage.
About four miles above the La Bahia crossing, on the
East side of the Colorado, commence the pine forests,
extending above Bastrop; affording to this region of
country great convenience in respect of good timber.
On the West side of the river again, about one and a
half miles above the same crossing, the prairie approach-

13

es immediately up to the margin of the river, elevated above its ordinary surface about eighty feet, and secured for near a mile by a fine bluff of rock.

Immediately East of Colorado city,* on the lower side of Buckner's creek, rise Buckner's heights, a beautiful range of hills, about three hundred feet in height above the surrounding plain. The side towards the river is almost perpendicular. The plain on the summit of these heights is of surpassing beauty, and the surrounding prospect, as far as vision can extend, as rich as Nature presents. Immediately below lies the fertile plain of Colorado city, sprinkled over with clusters of live oak and small islands of timber. Towards the South-west and West, sweep away in the distant horizon, the high, dry and undulating Navidad prairies, resembling some mighty bay or arm of the sea. To the North-west, the serpentine meanderings of Buckner's creek and the Colorado river, as they approximate in the distance towards the mountains, are distinctly marked out by the dark line of forest which generally clothe their margins. The Colorado mountains also lend their aid to variegate the scene, lifting their lofty summits above the neighboring country. The evergreen pine imparts a solemn richness to the landscape, extending far up the country.

On the summits of Buckner's heights, are found numerous pure cool fountains of living water, which in beautiful rivulets approach each other, until, blended together, they reach the brow of the cliff opposite Colorado city, and precipitate their waters over in a cas-

* See page 151.

cade of twenty-five feet, and thence, leaping from rock to rock, make their way down to Buckner's creek.

*Gonzales,* the county seat of a county of the same name, is handsomely situated on the East bank of the Guadaloupe, sixty-five miles from the Gulf, and forty-five from the mountains. It was one of the most flourishing towns in Texas before the war, was the centre of an extensive trade, and had many fine edifices. It was burnt by the Texan army when it retreated to the Colorado, March 10th, 1836; since, it has continued almost entirely desolate.

The surrounding country presents an almost continued series of rolling prairies, gently undulating at the South, but swelling into high bold eminences at the North. The soil, along the Guadaloupe and La Baca, is of a rich black mould, remarkably fertile and productive; and between these streams it is intermixed with sand in many places, which renders it less compact and stiff, but not less productive. Cotton, sugar cane, corn, potatoes, wheat, rye, oats, &c., are produced here in abundance. Live oak, post oak, Spanish oak, elm, ash, black walnut, cypress, and musquit prevail.

*Bexar* is situated on both sides of the Rio San Antonio, about twenty miles above its junction with the Medina, in latitude 29 deg. 26 min., longitude 21 deg. 38 min. The plan of the town is that of an oblong square, from which streets extend at right angles. The houses are built of a kind of free-stone; are all one story high, and covered with flat roofs, over which a parapet is raised about two and a half feet, giving the whole the appearance of an extensive fortification. In the centre of the public square—which, as in the case of other Spanish towns, is the central point from which the streets run at right angles—are some large houses and a very ancient church, upon which Gen. Cos, when occupying Bexar in '35, caused a platform to be erected, and, upon it, artillery to be planted.

Bexar is one of the oldest towns in North America,* containing many ancient structures, which recall to mind its former greatness, and the many vicissitudes of fortune which have characterized its singular and interesting history. It contained, a few years since, eight or ten thousand inhabitants : the present population is only about one thousand. Nature seems to have destined it to become one of the first cities in America.

The Alamo is situated at the North-east part of the town, on the left bank of the San Antonio. It is a large, oblong, walled enclosure, containing about an acre of ground ; the wall is about eight or ten feet high and three feet thick. Since the fall of Travis and his heroic band, it has been dismantled ; and no longer a fortress, it remains only to designate the Thermopylæ of Texas.

Below Bexar, and scattered along the banks of the San Antonio, are many beautiful edifices, built of massive stone, styled Missions, generally consisting of a fortress and a church.

Some of these churches are of a very imposing appearance ; sufficiently large to contain six hundred or seven hundred people, and covered with lofty arched roofs of stone. Formerly, they were surmounted with

* Founded in 1692.

enormous bells, and ornamented with numerous carved statues and paintings. The entrance to the Mission of Espada is by a magnificent arched gateway, through which six horsemen may ride abreast. During a century and a half, these Missions, as well as the towns of Bexar and Goliad, have been repeatedly plundered, and attempts made to destroy them, but in vain. In them the pious fathers of former days, with the sword in one hand and the Bible in the other, gathered the wild bands of the prairie to bend the knee to the shrine of the Virgin.

The climate of this region is delightful, and probably not surpassed by that of any portion of the globe. The summers are never oppressively warm, but are admirably tempered by cool, refreshing sea-breezes, which prevail during the warm season. The winters are exceedingly mild, pleasant and comfortable. Snow hardly ever falls, even to the depth of an inch; and although most of the rainy weather is in the winter, there are but very few cloudy days. Indeed, such is the salubrity of the climate, that, previous to the war, there were many Mexicans who had resided in the vicinity of Bexar for more than a century in perfect health.

## MINOR TOWNS.

Besides the interior towns, now described, which are, or have been, of the most importance in Texas, there are several others which demand a passing notice, as well as the country adjacent to them.

*San Patricio* is situated in a delightful prairie, on the North-east bank of the Nueces, about seven miles

13*

above its mouth.   It was formerly a place of considerable importance, and contained forty or fifty houses.
It is now almost entirely deserted.

The surrounding country, with the exception of narrow belts of wood-land along the streams, is a vast prairie ; diversified by a few insulated groves of musquit,
post-oak, and a tall shrub called wisatchy.   The soil is
generally poor and sandy ; near the Nueces, Colorado,
and Rio Grande, however, at a distance from the coast,
it is excellent, consisting generally of a rich alluvial
deposite of reddish loam, or a deep black sandy mould,
intermixed with dark colored sand.   This region is far
from being the desert it has been generally represented.
Most of it supports a dense mat of grass, and is admirably adapted to pasturage.   It is one of the most
healthy portions of Texas : the climate is arid and
mild.   It is now almost depopulated, the consequence
of border warfare.

*Lipantitlan* is situated on the South-west side of the
Nueces, about four miles above San Patricio, in the
woody fringe of the river.   It formerly contained about
forty houses, and was reputed a very healthy and beautiful village.

*Goliad* is situated on the right bank of the San Antonio river, about thirty or thirty-five miles from its
mouth.   It is, next to Bexar, the oldest town in Texas,
founded in 1716.   Its site, on the margin of an extensive prairie, though rocky, is pleasant and healthy.
The soil of the surrounding country is generally a dark
sandy loam, easily worked, and very productive.   Goliad is now nearly desolate.

*Victoria* is situated on the left bank of the Guada-

loupe, about twenty or twenty-five miles above its junction with the San Antonio.    The surrounding country
is generally prairie ;  its soil, a rich sandy loam.

*Texana*, a county seat, is situated on the right bank
of the Navidad, at the head of steamboat navigation.    Its site is partly within the bordering forest of
the Navidad, and partly within a beautiful prairie, extending Westerly several miles, to the woody fringe of
the La Baca.    Texana is yet quite a small town, containing only fifteen or twenty houses ; but its commanding situation must eventually render it a principal inland town of Texas.    The soil of the surrounding country is exceedingly rich and productive, consisting of a
layer of black mould, generally two or three feet deep.

This section of country has now a small population,
thinly scattered over its surface.    A large number of
most excellent farms have remained wholly unimproved
since the fall of the Alamo.    The former planters,
however, are slowly returning to their homes, accompanied by hundreds of enterprizing settlers from the
United States, whose industry and perseverance are
rapidly removing the remaining vestiges of the war.

*Colorado City* is situated upon a romantic ¦bluff, already described, on the West bank of the Colorado river, about one and a half miles above the La Bahia
Crossing.    About five hundred acres of the bluff, on
which is the site of this town, were purchased by a Company a year since, and the town laid off : an undivided
interest in which has already been sold at an advance
of seven hundred per cent. ; and nine hundred per cent.
advance offered for one-sixteenth of the remainder.

Receding from the river, the site of Colorado City

rises beautifully to the height of thirty feet above the front plane. Nature has lavishly supplied it with four springs of excellent water; one of which is so considerable as to have suggested to the proprietors of the town the idea of placing a small mill upon it. Five or six miles West, in the direction of Buckner's Creek, rises a beautiful mineral spring, which, in its sulphurous smell and white deposite, much resembles the celebrated White Sulphur Springs of Virginia.

On account of the very desirable location of Colorado City in other respects—elevated and airy, upon a plane of gentle declivity, and a sandy soil, forbidding the apprehension of muddy streets, with an abundance of excellent building material in its neighborhood, pine timber above and rock beneath on the river—it will very probably rival, if not surpass, Bastrop, particularly should it become the permanent Seat of Government of the Republic.

*Columbus*, a county seat, is pleasantly situated on the West bank of the Colorado river, about sixty miles from its mouth. Its site is upon a high bluff, forming a part of a beautiful prairie, surrounded by dense forests of live oak and cotton wood. It is yet quite a small village, containing about twenty houses.

The adjacent country, to the South, is level; to the North, gently undulating. A broad, open prairie extends from the fringing woods of the Colorado to the bottoms of the San Banard, East; and a similar prairie from the Colorado, westerly, to the woody fringe of the Navidad. These prairies, like most of the low country of Texas, are intersected by deep ravines, worn by small streams, through the deep bed of reddish

loam which extends many miles on each side of the
Colorado. Towards the San Banard, these ravines
are rather shallow, owing to the quantity of sand intermixed with the loam. The soil is generally fertile ;
near the Colorado and Navidad it is excellent, consisting of a rich black mould, resting on a reddish loam ;
in the neighborhood of the San Banard it is sandy,
and not very productive.

*La Grange* is situated on the East bank of the Colorado river, at the La Bahia Crossing. The surrounding country affords an inexhaustible supply of the best
building material. Pine, cedar, and other valuable
timber, is abundant ; and also a very valuable species
of rock, which is easily worked, and becomes harder
by exposure to the atmosphere. In its immediate neighborhood are many rivulets of clear running water, on
which are sites for mills and other machinery. The
soil, climate and scenery of the surrounding country
have been already described.

*Monticello* is a town site on the West bank of the
Brazos, about sixty miles from its mouth. It is in the
live oak region of Texas, is open to the sea-breeze, and
commands a view of a verdant and beautiful prairie.
The adjacent country has been already sufficiently described.

*Nashville* and *Tenoxticlan*, on the Upper Brazos, are
destined to be towns of some importance. The surrounding country is comparatively healthy, and very
fertile, and promises soon to be densely populated.

*Richmond* is situated upon an elevated, beautiful prairie on the West bank of the Brazos, about seventy miles
from its mouth. It is, at present, a place of little im-

portance, but promises to become one of the largest inland towns of Texas. The surrounding country is very fertile and productive.

*Bolivar*, like Richmond, little more than a town in name, is situated on the East bank of the Brazos, about sixty miles from its mouth. It is generally considered as the head of tide-water and of navigation. In the surrounding country are considerable improvements, and an exuberant soil.

*Harrisburgh* was a town of some importance before the war. It is situated on the right bank of Buffalo Bayou. It was burnt by the army under Santa Anna, just before the battle of San Jacinto. The adjacent country is generally sandy and unproductive.

*Liberty* is very pleasantly situated on the East side of the Trinity River, about thirty miles from its mouth. It contains ten or twelve houses, and is surrounded by many fine farms. The soil of the adjacent country is generally light and sandy, except upon the Trinity, where it is excellent.

*Lynchburgh*, situated near the junction of Buffalo Bayou and the San Jacinto, is of late date and little importance. The surrounding country is generally prairie, or covered with a valuable growth of pine. It is moderately productive.

*Anahuac* is very pleasantly situated on the North-eastern part of Galveston Bay, a little below the mouth of the Trinity. It is memorable for the difficulties which occurred there in 1832 and '35. It was select-ed in 1830, by Col. Bradburn, as a military post, and occupied as such under the Mexican Government down to 1835. It contains about sixty houses, most of which are vacant.   The soil of the surrounding country is light and sandy.

*New Washington* is situated near the head of Galveston Bay, a little below the mouth of the San Jacinto. "Nature, by the diversity of its scenery, the tesselated declivity, gently ascending from the Bay, and studded with young trees, the invigorating sea-breeze from the Bay on the one side, and the delightful vista of the San Jacinto River, in all its meanderings, on the other, the thick foliage of the forest, in its compact insulation, relieving the monotony of the prairie : all these natural advantages proclaim New Washington to be the site of some future emporium of commerce." It was burnt by the army under Santa Anna in the spring of '36, and is now a town only in name.

*Liverpool* is a town site on the West bank of the Chocolate Bayou, about twenty miles, by water, from its mouth, forty-five from the city of Galveston, and thirteen, by a direct course, from the river Brazos.

*Buffalo* is a town site on Buffalo Bayou, eight miles distant from Houston, ten miles from the mouth of the San Jacinto, and twenty-two miles from the Brazos. The adjacent country is well timbered, and tolerably productive.

*Jasper* is situated on the West bank of Sandy Creek, in an extensive plain.   It contains about twelve or fourteen houses.   In the vicinity are many excellent farms.   The surrounding country is generally poor.

*Jefferson*, a county seat, is situated on the East bank, and at the head of navigation, on Cow Creek.   It is surrounded by many good farms, and contains about a dozen houses.   The adjacent country is very generally

level prairie, of a poor soil, and embraces some extensive swamps.   The soil upon the Neches, however,
and other neighboring water-courses, is excellent, consisting of a black sandy mould, resting on a bed of yel-
low clay, intermixed with sand.   The swamps may be
very profitably cultivated in rice.

*Montgomery* is situated in the county of Washington,
sixty miles North-west of the city of Houston, thirty-
five miles East of the town of Washington, and six
miles West of the San Jacinto river, in a high, pleasant and undulating country, distinguished for health
and good water.

The San Jacinto affords an excellent steamboat navigation to this point.   The most direct routes from the
city of Houston to Robertson's Colony and the Red River Settlements, and from Bevil's Settlement to Washington, pass through this town.   The great extent of
good land contiguous, and an increasing agricultural
population, cannot fail to make this a town of importance.

*Hamilton* is pleasantly situated on the left bank of
Buffalo Bayou, opposite the town of Harrisburgh.   It
is five miles from the city of Houston, the present Seat
of Government, and possesses decided advantages as a
commercial point.   In its neighborhood is an abundance of pine, cypress, cedar, and oak timber.

*San Leon* is a town site, upon a high and beautiful
bluff, on the West side of Galveston Bay, immediately
at the commencement of Red-fish Bar.   It is not exposed to inundation, has good water, and is healthy.

As the towns now described are, with few exceptions, upon water-courses, the reader may suppose that

the accompanying descriptions of sections of country adjacent, apply altogether or mostly to bottom lands. Such application has been by no means intended, but, on the contrary, an application to a section of country equi-distant on all sides, and co-extensive generally with the limits of counties. It should be observed, however, that whilst the bottom lands are generally skirted with timber, the intermediate country is more generally prairie, and that the prairie is not so uniformly fertile as the timbered bottoms; yet it must by no means be supposed that the prairies are generally, or in any considerable degree, a waste. In some places, near the seaboard, and to the West, they are nearly so; but, generally, they consist, in the lower country, of a deep, black mould, resting upon a substratum of loam, which is also deep and free from stones. In the upper country, they generally consist of a dark, deep, sandy loam.

These remarks are, of course, of general application. The writer supposes that he has already otherwise sufficiently described the soil and surface of the country.

## SEA-BOARD TOWNS.

### *Commercial Advantages, Bays, Harbors, &c.*

The writer has felt a peculiar interest in canvassing all questions relating to the harbors, commercial towns, and commercial advantages of Texas. The commerce of a country like Texas, with an extensive sea-board and an enterprizing population, is of scarce less importance than her soil. With commerce, she is to hold intercourse with the great family of man; have brought

14

to her citizens the intelligence which moves in the common mass of mind—to her tables, the luxuries of other climes—to her coffers, gold—to her borders, strength—and to herself, a *name*, as well as a place, among the nations. Let us see, then, how she is situated in respect of commerce. In the first place, she has a sea-board of about four hundred miles in extent; lies convenient for trade with the United States, with the West Indies, with Mexico and South America, as well as Europe; her coast is interspersed with several fine bays, and at convenient distances from each other; and she may, and no doubt will, have an interior country both to demand and support an extensive trade. But yet she has difficulties to contend-with, and they must be fairly stated. In the first place, her coast is low, and liable to occasional and partial inundation; the inlets to her bays and harbors are shallow; and many of her harbors not good. Ingenuity, enterprize, and industry, combined with wealth, will, doubtless, lessen these evils; but still they must, in a great measure, remain. Can Texas, then, carry on an extensive foreign commerce?

*Galveston*, though not central to the sea-board of Texas, may be made, by means of railroads of moderate extent, the depot for the produce of the most fertile sections of the interior of the Republic; and, of course, the point from which goods, imported from abroad, may be readily distributed where most wanted. On the bar at the entrance of the harbor, are ordinarily from twelve to thirteen feet of water, and at the highest tides from thirteen to seventeen. Vessels, then, of from 250 to 350 tons burthen—according to their construction—can pass the bar. Such vessels are sufficiently large for a coast trade with the United States, Mexico, and South America, and also for the West India trade. Thus, then, is an extensive foreign commerce from Galveston certainly practicable. But for trade to Europe and other parts of the world, larger vessels, of 400 or 500 tons, may be desirable, if not necessary. Can such get into Galveston? It is believed that, as they are now generally constructed, they cannot. But can they not be differently constructed, and be equally safe and profitable? It is believed they can; and that thus Texas may carry on an extensive trade at least with Europe. This effected, a very considerable commercial importance will be secured to her—enough, perhaps, to meet all her wants until her citizens shall extend their improvements to the Pacific, and open there new channels of trade.

Galveston Island stretches along the Gulf of Mexico for about thirty miles, in nearly a North-easterly and South-westerly direction. Upon the most Eastern part is laid off the *City of Galveston.*

The harbor at this city is spacious, and sufficiently large for five hundred vessels to lie at anchor. Its immediate location is one of the most beautiful and healthy on the sea coast. It is considerably rising above the bay,—affords admirable ground for building and for good streets, and is well watered. Being continually fanned by the sea breeze, no climate can be more desirable and healthy than the city of Galveston.

This city commands the whole trade of the Trinity and San Jacinto rivers, and of Buffalo Bayou. And by means of a short railroad, fifteen miles long, from

Houston to *Fort Bend*, on the Brazos river, and by
a canal three and a half miles long, from Velasco, at
the mouth of the Brazos, to West Bay, which commu-
nicates with the harbor of Galveston,—the passage being sufficiently deep for any sort of steamboat navigation,—the whole trade of the heart of Texas, of all the
rich soil watered by the Brazos, and its thickly populated tributaries, will necessarily flow into the city of
Galveston for exportation. This is the great outlet
for the cotton trade of Texas. Nothing but small
craft can enter the mouth of the Brazos, or any other
port of Texas, while ships of three or four hundred tons
can load at Galveston with cotton for Liverpool or Ha-
vre. Nature has marked this spot out for a great commercial city. A railroad is contemplated to be made
from Houston to Washington, on the Brazos, fifty miles
in length, which will still more completely command
for Galveston the entire trade of the Brazos. And
another important railroad is contemplated to be made,
leading from the three forks on the Trinity river to Fort
Towson, or Pecan Point, on Red River, one hundred
and twenty miles in length.

The city of Galveston will also, without doubt, command the trade of the Sabine and the Neches rivers,
by a canal one and a half miles long, joining East Galveston Bay with Sabine Lake, through Taylor's and
East Bay Bayous, which are both broad and deep. The
outlet of Sabine Lake into the Gulf can never be of
the least importance, as no more than four or five
feet of water can possibly be obtained at any time
on the bar.

To the North sweeps away in a distance of thirty

miles, the magnificent *Bay of Galveston*. This bay may be of an average width of twelve miles; has upon its shores several desirable sites for towns, and in its waters an inexhaustible supply of fish and oysters; and though its navigation is a good deal obstructed by bars, yet steamboats of sufficient size for purposes of transportation, if rightly constructed, can at all times pass its entire length.

In this bay, a year since, there were two steamboats—now there are not less than six or seven; then there were, at times, eight or ten sail of vessels—within the last few months there have been not unfrequently from twenty to twenty-five; then, the customs of the port might have been five or six thousand per quarter—now, they are not less than fifty thousand.

Galveston City is yet in its infancy, though rapidly improving. It contains about thirty or forty considerable buildings.

*Velasco* and *Quintana* are towns nearly opposite, at the mouth of the Brazos. Velasco is the oldest and most important place, and, owing to the more enterprizing character of its population, is likely to continue so. It is situated on the East bank of the Brazos, mostly upon a sandy beach. Its site, open to the sea, is healthy, and pleasant to such as like to look upon the " expanse of waters," and to hear the " deep resounding main."

The importance of Velasco, in point of trade,—as is, and will continue to be, the case with most of the towns in Texas, until internal improvements shall have fixed their rank,—is very questionable. It may be the point at which will be received the future immense products

14*

of the navigable, and more than the navigable, waters of the Brazos, and at which goods will be received to supply the inhabitants of the country along those waters.  If so, it will become a town of the first magnitude in Texas ; but if, on the contrary, by railroads or canals, a great part of the produce of the country upon the Brazos should be taken to Galveston, Velasco can, at most, be but a town of secondary importance.  In any event, the trade at the place will have to contend, probably always, with the great obstacle of a bar at the mouth of the river, upon which there is not ordinarily more than six and a half feet of water.  Besides, the approach of vessels is often rendered hazardous by a heavy rolling surf; and their departure from the port is very liable to be impeded, during a large portion of the year, by head winds.

Velasco, however, as a place of residence, has many decided advantages.  It may be supplied at all times with excellent fish, and in almost any quantity.  The writer has himself assisted in hauling the seine upon the beach, containing a " multitude of fishes," among which were forty red fish and several trout.  Oysters may be found, at no great distance, in abundance.  The great luxury of sea-bathing is at no place more convenient, safe, and pleasant : one may find water deep or shallow, to his mind, and every where a smooth, hard beach.  Velasco contains about twenty-five or thirty considerable buildings and one hundred and fifty or two hundred inhabitants, and the largest hotel in Texas.

*Matagorda*, at present the most important sea-board town in Texas, is situated on the left bank and at the mouth of the river Colorado.  At a point nearly central to the sea-board of Texas, upon the shores of an expansive and beautiful bay, and at the mouth of a river which flows through a country scarcely less productive than that upon the Brazos, Matagorda will doubtless be the depot of an extensive trade ; and, but for the shoal water of the bay, which prevents the larger class of vessels which can pass the bar at Passo Cavallo from approaching within a mile of it, would probably be the future emporium of the commerce of Texas. Its site is upon a prairie bluff, elevated and healthy. It contains about five hundred inhabitants, and is rapidly improving.

*Matagorda Bay* receives the waters of the Colorado, Navidad, and La Baca rivers. It is about thirty miles in length, from East to West, and of very irregular outline. Its shores are generally elevated, and afford several very desirable sites for towns ; some of which—particularly one called Austin—are said to be accessible by all vessels which can pass the bar at Passo Cavallo.

*Cox's Point*, at present little more than a landing, is on the North-western shore of Matagorda Bay, at the mouth of the La Baca and Navidad rivers. Its site is pleasant and healthy, and it promises to be a place of considerable importance. It is accessible by vessels which can pass the bar at Passo Cavallo.

*Copano*, upon Aransaso Bay, is at present attracting a good deal of attention. Its site is elevated and healthy, and is said to be quite picturesque and beautiful. It is accessible by all vessels which can cross the bar at the inlet of the bay. Upon this bar there are seven or eight feet of water at ordinary tides. Improvements, just now beginning at Copano, will undoubtedly progress with great rapidity. Besides a considerable trade with Western Texas, of which it will be the depot, Copano will have some peculiar advantages for carrying on a trade with Mexico, which is destined to be exceedingly profitable.

## PROSPECTIVE TRADE OF TEXAS.

Upon a review of what has now been said of the commercial advantages of Texas, and a cast of the eye at the map of the same, the reader must admit that those advantages are considerable, and inviting to the enterprizing merchant. But the account of the prospective trade of Texas is yet but half presented. In giving the remaining half, however, the writer, lest he should seem to run into unwarrantable speculation, will be very brief. It is yet to be ascertained whether Texas will not be able to establish such relations with some of the European powers, particularly Great Britain,* as will afford her very great and peculiar advantages. Such relations once established, it is believed that her product in cotton alone, which may be made equal to that of the United States, will enable her to sustain them exceedingly to her own interest. This effected—without speculating upon the probability of her extending her territory, so as to embrace the now Northern States of Mexico, to the 26th parallel of latitude inclusive between the two oceans, and her citizens having thus a very extensive region to supply—she will

---

* By late advices from England, it appears that a treaty of trade has been effected with the Government of that country by the Texan Envoy.

doubtless eventually be able at least to monopolize the now extensive and profitable trade which is carried on between the United States and the interior of Mexico by caravans from Missouri. Without statistical statements in proof, the reader, at all acquainted with that trade, may be convinced of the fact by a glance of the eye at the map of Texas, Mexico, and the United States. It should be stated, however, that, with the exception of the intervening mountainous region, of no great extent, such is the surface of the country between the navigable waters, and even the Western sea-board of Texas and New Mexico, as to afford excellent roads for transportation, without other labor or expense bestowed upon them than the establishment of ferries and the construction of necessary bridges.

## PRODUCTS.

*Cotton* is doubtless to be the great staple of Texas : sufficient has been said of it, in the general, already. Some particulars of its quality, and the quantity which can be raised to the hand and the acre, remain only now to be stated.

The Texas cotton is allowed, in the New Orleans market at least, if not the European, to be superior in quality to that generally produced in the United States ; and the former commands from one to two cents per pound more than the latter. This is a fact ; for which, if a reason were demanded, it would be sufficient to say, that the difference in the quality of the cotton is owing as well to the great difference in the climate, as the soil, of Texas and the United States. A cotton planter

of Alabama, not long since in Texas, says he believes
that Sea Island cotton will produce well two hundred
miles interior ; that near the " cross timbers" there is a
saline atmosphere, and saline plants are found, caused
by great quantities of salt on the surface of the earth
in that region.

In Texas, it has been repeatedly stated that ten bales
of cotton may be made to the hand, and that a hand
will clear, upon an opened plantation, four or five hundred dollars per annum.    Indeed, it seems to be the
opinion of the best judges, that, on a good soil, and
under favorable circumstances, two and a half bales
may be made to the acre, which would, in Texas, be
from eight to ten bales to the hand.    On an average,
however, it is believed that not more than a bale and a
half can be made to the acre, which might be about
five or six bales to the hand.

*Sugar.*—Of this, as a product of Texas, little can yet
be said, except in anticipation.  If a comparison be
instituted between Texas and Louisiana, in respect of
climate and latitude, it will appear that the former has
the advantage of the latter as a sugar country.    In the
first place, Texas has a large extent of sea-board, along
which sweep the trade winds, with little interruption,
for six or seven months in the year, rendering the climate, during that time especially, equable and mild, and
preventing late spring and early autumnal frosts, thus
rendering the sugar-cane little liable to injury at these
seasons of the year.    In Louisiana, late and early frosts
are the great obstacle to a good crop of sugar.  Again,
a considerable part of the sea-board of Texas lies somewhat South of Louisiana, which, little as the difference

may be, is evidently an advantage in favor of the former for the growth of sugar-cane. This will be the more evident, when the fact is considered, that at "le Grand Terre," and other places in the South-western part of Louisiana, sugar-cane often *flowers*, which it scarcely ever does in those parts where it is more generally planted. This, though it should be as well the effect of the contiguity of the places mentioned to the sea, as of latitude, is not the less an important fact in a comparison of Texas with Louisiana in respect to the growth of sugar-cane. In point of soil, there can be no question that a large part of that upon the sea-board of Texas is equally fertile, and equally well adapted to sugar, as that of Louisiana.

*The Vine.*—On account of its geograpical position, and the character of its soil and climate, Texas is destined to become the vineyard of North America. Almost every variety of grape, and of delicious flavor, is found growing spontaneously in many parts, particularly about Nacogdoches, in the neighborhood of Bastrop, and along the watres of the Guadaloupe. Some of these native grapes are said to yield a wine similar to the best Oporto. It is believed—indeed, there can be no doubt—that the valuable grapes of Europe may be introduced into Texas to great advantage.

*Silk.*—It is certain that in Texas, especially the Western part, silk may be produced to more advantage than in most, if not any part of the United States. The reasons are the following: 1st, In Western Texas rain falls but seldom, and almost never in driving, beating storms; indeed, in an agricultural point of view, the want of sufficient rain is an objection to Western

Texas, the planter there having to adopt, to some extent, an artificial method of irrigating his land. This, which to agriculture is an evil, is a decided advantage in the production of silk. 2dly, The mulberry tree grows remarkably well in the West of Texas. And, 3dly, An experiment in the production of silk has been tried at San Antonio de Bexar, whilst it was under the Spanish Government, and proved remarkably successful. The writer has seen a statement of the comparative profits of labor and capital employed in the production of silk, and that of corn and other grains, in the New England States, and, if he mistakes not, it was as 400 to 1. If, then, in New England, silk can be produced at such a profit, what will be the result of its production in Texas, when it is considered especially that the transportation of the raw material to any part of the globe,—if it cannot be profitably manufactured in Texas,—will be attended with trifling expense.

*Wheat.*—Though Texas cannot be said to be generally adapted to the growth of wheat, yet, by experiment in the neighborhood of Bexar, on the Upper Colorado, it has been ascertained that the Mexican wheat, which is superior to that raised in the United States, will, in those, and of course must in similar, sections of the country, do very well.

*Fruits.*—The Fig, a very delicious and exceedingly valuable fruit, is well adapted to the climate of Texas, and, with very little labor and attention, may be raised in the greatest abundance.

Melons grow to a great size, are very abundant, and of a delicious flavor.

The Quince, a very valuable fruit, is said to produce remarkably well in Texas.

The Peach is no where better than in Texas. Indeed, in size and flavor, the Texas peach is believed to be unrivalled : the so-much celebrated Jersey peach, found in the Philadelphia and New-York markets, will not compare with it.    In Texas, moreover, the peach is scarcely ever injured by frost, and requires but little attention.

Plums of various kinds may be produced abundantly.

The Apricot is adapted to the climate of Texas.

Oranges, it is believed, may be raised in abundance in the Southern and Western parts.

The abundance of native Grapes in Texas has already been mentioned.    Indeed, with the exception of the apple, there is scarcely any fruit common at the North, which will not grow abundantly in Texas.

The Prickly Pear is a wild native fruit of the country, growing abundantly upon the sea-board.    It is pleasant to the taste, and its leaves, which are very large, some a foot and a half wide, are valuable for their medicinal qualities.    It is remarkable that the Coat of Arms of Mexico is a prickly pear tree, with an eagle perched upon it ; and more remarkable, that the manner of the division of Mexico into States, is that of the leaves of the prickly pear springing from their stock.

*Game* is yet abundant in Texas.    One accustomed to the use of the rifle may, in almost any part of the country, keep a table well supplied with excellent venison.    Deer abound upon the prairies.    Wild turkies are numerous, generally fat, and their meat tender and delicious.    Several of them may at times be seen perched upon a fence, even in the neighborhood of a

15

house. Prairie hens, a large fine bird, and generally fat, are very plenty. Bears, the meat of which is esteemed excellent, are very common. Buffalo also abound in many parts.

*Stock.*—There is nothing for which Texas affords such superlative advantages over most other countries as the raising of stock. Her boundless prairies are her pastures and her meadows, already prepared by the hand of Nature, covered every where with grass, and in many parts with that of a very superior kind. Indeed, to one wishing to grow rich in the most quiet, easy, delightful, and certain manner, there is no business so inviting as raising stock in Texas. Such is the mild. ness of the climate, that cattle, horses, hogs, sheep, and other animals, can obtain a subsistence, and generally even keep fat, during the entire winter in the prairies. Hence, all the great labor and expense necessary to the farmer of the North, to subsist his cattle during the winter, is in Texas wholly unnecessary. The Texan farmer has only to brand his stock when young, and turn it loose, and, with the exception of such as he works, it requires no farther attention, save that occasionally of the herdsman to salt it, and see that it does not wander to too great a distance.

The horned cattle and hogs of Texas are especially large and fine looking; they increase, particularly the latter, with astonishing rapidity—so much so, that in the course of eight or ten years the Texan farmer may become rich by these animals alone, and almost without having known what it is to labor. There can be no reason why sheep, especially in the Northern and Western parts of Texas, may not be raised in count-

less numbers, and to nearly as great advantage as cattle; for though their wool should not be as fine and
as valuable as that of Northern sheep, their meat is
peculiarly tender, and of delicate flavor.

The writer has not intended to remark particularly
in respect to all the domestic animals, nor all the products of Texas, but such only as present something of
peculiar interest. It may be unnecessary to say, that
corn, rye, oats, potatoes, &c., produce as well in Texas
as in the Southern and South-western States.

## MINERALS.

*Silver* is said to have been found in many parts of
Texas, and there is no good reason to doubt it; but it
is known, that on or near the San Saba, which empties
into the Colorado about sixty miles above Bastrop,
there is a silver mine of great value. This mine was
formerly worked whilst Mexico was under the dominion of Old Spain, and afforded a considerable revenue
to the Spanish crown. It is on record in the archives
of Mexico, as of the third quality wrought within the
boundaries of New Spain. More recently, it would
seem, there has been discovered at this mine an extensive vein of very pure silver, of which, it is said, the
neighboring Camanches make bullets as of lead. This
mine is beginning to excite very considerable attention
in Texas. A company was about forming at Houston,
in the spring of the present year, for the purpose of
exploring it, and others said to be in the neighborhood.
They would long since have been explored but for the
peril of the adventure. The Camanches are exceed-

ingly jealous of the appearance of a white man about them—not so much for any value they attach to the mines, as the prospect of a permanent inroad upon their dominions, if white men are allowed to work them.

*Iron Ore* is found in abundance in the Eastern, Northern, and Middle portions of Texas. Upon the upper waters of the Trinity, vast quantities of this ore have lately been discovered, said to contain fifty per cent. of iron.

*Bituminous Coal* is found extensively in the region of the Upper Colorado, said to be equal to the Pittsburgh coal.

*Salt* is found in the greatest abundance. There is a famous salt lake about thirty miles East of the Rio Grande, and seventy miles from San Patricio. This lake, or rather pond, is about three miles in circumference, and of an oval figure. Its waters generally evaporate during the summer, leaving its bed completely covered by a crust of salt four or five inches thick. Immense quantities of this salt are annually collected by the Mexicans of the neighboring States. During the dry season it is collected by breaking the crust into large cakes, and in the wet season the cubical crystals are raked together from the bottom into baskets, and in this manner taken away. There are several other salt lakes, of less importance, numerous salt springs, and even salt rivers, in Texas.

*Lead, copper, copperas,* and *alum,* are found in considerable quantities.

The bed of the Colorado is paved with a large number of siliceous minerals ; among which are found agate, chalcedony, and a few singular petrifactions.

Remarkably large *Petrifactions* are found in many places.   On the Trinity, near " Robertson's," is a tree about thirty feet long and three feet over, perfectly petrified.   Besides this, in the same neighborhood, are many other petrifactions.   Near the Brazos, in Austin's Colony, is a large stump of a tree perfectly petrified.

The mineral which has, more than any other which he has seen in Texas, interested the writer, on account particularly of its great value as a building material, is a species of *free-stone,* found near Bexar.   It is, when first taken from the quarry, quite soft, and may be whittled with a penknife as easily as a bit of soft wood ; but, upon exposure to the atmosphere, becomes so hard that cannon balls can make little or no impression upon it, and seems to be as little liable to decay as marble or granite.   In a country like Texas, where a cool house is particularly desirable in summer, this stone, which is thus durable, and which is very easily worked, must be exceedingly valuable for purposes of building.

## MINERAL SPRINGS.

Twenty-five miles from Washington is a large Sulphur Spring, covering a surface of about twenty feet square, the bottom of which is perfectly white, and the water blue.   It was once sold, with the half or quarter league of land on which it is, for five hundred dollars ; again, for five thousand ; and since, thirty thousand dollars have been refused for it.

Near the Sibolo, and about thirty-three miles from Bexar, is a Mineral Spring, the waters of which have
**15***

for ages been held in high estimation by the aborigines for their medicinal qualities. Besides these, and the one already mentioned near Colorado city, there are several other Mineral Springs in Texas, which promise to be very valuable.

## TIMBER.

It has been often asserted by the planter of the South and West of the States, that lands in Texas can be of but little value, for the want of timber. It is a question first asked, "What will you do for fencing?" And then, "What will you do for building material and fuel?"

Now, in the first place, timber is not so very scarce in Texas as some have represented, and many believed. There is sufficient for purposes of building for a long time to come ; and though it will not be found convenient to all places where it will be in demand, yet its transportation, in a country like Texas, will be attended with little expense. And, besides, comparatively little will be wanted for building ; the many barns, sheds, &c., common and necessary at the North, are not needed in Texas.

For fuel—little of which is wanted in Texas, fires being necessary only about three months of the year— there is, with few exceptions, plenty of timber for the present ; and the future may be provided for, by planting certain trees, which grow with great rapidity and make the best of fuel. But, in addition to this, Texas will doubtless be, ere long, to a considerable extent, supplied with fuel from her mines of coal.

In the second place, though for purposes of fencing it is admitted there is a scarcity of timber in Texas, yet the evil, if it be one at all, may be very easily, and, in the end, very profitably, remedied by hedges. Several species of thorn are found growing spontaneously, which may be planted at little expense of time and labor, and which will, in four or five years, grow to a sufficient size to make a good fence. Indeed, it is admitted, as the writer believes, generally, that in more Northern countries the hedge is in the end the cheapest, and in every way the best sort of fence; whilst, at the same time, it is an ornament to a landscape. Much more will this be the case in Texas, where the material for hedging is more abundant and varied, and grows more rapidly. Let, then, the planter erect his house upon the border of a woodland, where, for fuel and other purposes, it will be desirable to build, and first cultivate those portions of his land which are most convenient to timber, and which may be thus easily fenced; and, at the same time, along his fence plant his hedge; and, by the time his first fence is decayed, his hedge will supply its place; and as he progresses in the cultivation of his land, let him hedge in proportion—which he can do at times when he cannot very profitably employ his force otherwise—and so, by the time he has his plantation well improved in other respects, he will have it well hedged.

But, in the third place, why may it not be for the interest of the planter in Texas, who will generally be a raiser of stock to a considerable extent, to keep it restrained by means of herdsmen and dogs? This is done very much in Europe and other parts of the world, and the expense of fencing avoided—an expense, by the way, as fences are generally made in the United States, of very great account. The time and labor expended, particularly in the South and West, in preparing rails and constructing fences round large fields of cotton and corn, is immense.

Something, and perhaps enough, has already been said, of the different kinds of timber found in the different parts of Texas which have been described. In addition, and in general, it may be stated, that there are various species of oak found in abundance, particularly the live oak. Of this valuable timber, a greater amount is found in Texas than in any other known portion of the American continent of equal extent; indeed, according to a late estimate, something like a fourth part of the live oak upon the entire globe is in Texas. Pine, cypress, cedar, ash, elm, and other kinds of valuable timber, are also found in abundance in different parts. The India Rubber tree has been lately discovered, and is abundant upon the timber lands on the river Colorado, a few miles from Bastrop.


## PRAIRIES.

Though the proportion of prairie land, in Texas, is doubtless greater than is desirable for general purposes of agriculture, yet it presents great and decided advantages. As already remarked, the prairies are natural pastures of Texas, ready for the reception of the most extensive stock of the herdsman. The planter, who settles upon them, has not, in the first place, to spend an entire year in hard labor, preparing them for the first crop, and then, eventually, another year in order entirely to subdue them—as is necessary, for instance, for the planter on the Mississippi, in order to subdue his bottom lands—but has only to burn over his prairie to destroy the rank grass, immediately put in his plough, and plant his crop.

No pen can describe the varied beauties of these prairies in the spring of the year, when clothed, some in " living green," and some in flowers of a thousand hues, skirted with belts of timber, interspersed with groves, and covered almost with herds of deer: presenting the appearance of magnificent parks, tastefully laid out by the hand of man.

In every country, it may be, there is something of the sublime and beautiful. In New England, an example of the latter is the Connecticut, flowing along its fertile, wide-extended banks, covered with wheat, and corn, and meadows, with villages, hamlets and churches. In Virginia and other States, an example of the former, are the lofty rock-bound ridges, the deep chasms, and the precipitous cliffs of the Alleghanies. Another example of the same, in the " Great Valley," is the " Father of Waters," rolling majestically along his seemingly interminable forests. In Texas, the two are united in her vast prairies, sublime in extent and beautiful in prospect. Upon some of these, the traveller may move on for miles, and even leagues, over a continuous plain, with nothing to interrupt the utmost stretch of vision, save here and there a clump of trees, like islands in an expanse of water. On others, one may travel for hours over gentle undulations, rising upon swell succeeding swell, and still see swells before him, like the heavings of the majestic sea, with nothing to interrupt his admiration of the scene, save when the wild courser, startled, snuffs the air, and dashes away to some distant grove ; or the buffalo or deer bound over some neighboring swell. And if he chance to approach some lofty mound—the monument of the rude fore-fathers of the prairie—and ascends its height, like Moses of old on Pisgah's top, he beholds beneath him the "land of promise" in all its glory—beholds, extended wide, woodland and prairie, swells and plains, and meandering streams, and is "satisfied."

## RIVER SCENERY.

Upon the rivers of Texas, the Northerner finds himself in an entirely new scene. By day and by night, the water beneath and the sky above, as well as surrounding objects, present new and interesting features. The quiet, pellucid stream, which "like a mirror seems," reflecting the deep azure of the sky, the sun-beam and the forest, is itself a splendid panorama. The soil, the surface, the timber, fruits and flowers, of its banks, are to the Northerner all new ; new odors scent the air ; a strange melody greets the ear. Here and there, in a bend of the river, is an opening in the wood-land, and a verdant prairie extends to the river's brink, from which deer bound away, or upon which herds of wild cattle feed. Of a summer's night, upon these lovely streams, Nature appears in her sweetest, profoundest repose,— when the atmosphere is soft and bland, and all is silent, save when the fitful note of some wakeful bird, or the wolf's "long howl," strike the ear at intervals.

## TO THE MERCHANT.

The author has been often asked, since he has been in the United States, what articles will do well in Texas? What do the people want? And what will such and such articles sell for in Texas?

In the first place, and in general, it may be said, that, as the people of Texas are consumers of almost all kinds of foreign products, and as yet producers only to a very limited extent, all kinds of provisions which will keep in a warm climate are in constant demand in Texas.

The increase of the importation of provisions particularly, has, within the last year, greatly increased; but it has not been equal to the increasing demand, so great is the emigration to the country. During the last winter, provisions were much wanted in the interior, which could not be had. Flour, bacon, pork, lard, butter, cheese, sugar, molasses, rice, corn, and various preserved fruits, are most, and constantly, in demand. Various other articles, however, will doubtless, at times, do as well.

Most of the manufactures of the United States are wanted in Texas, particularly implements of husbandry, furniture, hard and earthen wares, boots, shoes, coarse cloths, nails, cordage, &c.

Lumber is, perhaps, in as great demand as any thing in Texas, and brings a very high price, from fifty to ninety dollars per thousand. Towns are increasing very rapidly in number and size; and though, for present purposes of building, sufficient lumber might be produced from the timber of the country, were it well supplied with saw-mills, yet labor is so much in demand, and wages so high in Texas, that at present, it is believed, that lumber may be imported from the United States at a less expense to the purchaser, at least upon the sea-board of Texas, than it could be had from saw-mills in the country. However this may be, in respect to lumber in its rough state, there can be little doubt that such as should be imported ready worked and fitted for building, could be afforded at a cheaper rate than could the same, or similar, prepared in the country from its native growth of timber.

It is frequently asked, " Why is every thing so high in Texas ?" And, " How can the people there afford to pay such prices ?" In answer to the first question, it may be said, that freight from New Orleans, where almost all supplies for Texas have been purchased, is exceedingly high ; import duties on many articles are high ; the rate of exchange has been much against Texas ; and, more than all, no one expects to do business in Texas at a less profit than from fifty to one hundred per cent.

In answer to the second question, it may be said, that the people of Texas cannot now afford the prices they pay for almost all articles of consumption, and that they are only, perhaps, generally, *able* to pay such prices by disposing of their surplus lands.

But this state of things, which is a great evil to Texas, will, it is believed, be soon remedied, not, perhaps, in the least by diminishing profits on trade, but, first, by means of a better currency, which Texas *may* have in a short time, and *must* have eventually. If the

Five Million Loan, which is now in the course of nego-
ciation with the United States Bank, is effected, Texas
will very soon have a good currency ; but, in the second
place, even if the loan is not effected, her valuable products must soon relieve her citizens of existing evils
in respect to their currency, and enable them also,
without feeling the expense, to purchase whatever they
want from abroad.

## TO MECHANICS.

Carpenters, bricklayers, blacksmiths, and, generally,
such other mechanics as find employment in the Southern States, can find plenty of work and the highest
wages in Texas. Let them take an abundance of tools,
go resolved to continue their industrious habits, to live
temperately and economically, and they will be certain
to accumulate wealth, to enjoy, in most places, their
usual, and, in many parts of the country, perhaps, more
than their usual, health.

## TO THE EMIGRANT.

Though Texas were quite the Eldorado it has been
by some represented, yet it would be desirable for the
emigrant, accustomed to the climate, institutions, man-
ners, habits, and customs of the Northern and Middle
States, to say nothing of foreign countries, to ascertain,
in the first place, as far as possible, whether he would
like those of the South ; and if, after due inquiry, or
personal observation,—which would be best,—he believes that he would, then he runs but little risk of dis-
appointment in removing to Texas.

16

Families emigrating should take along all the provisions they will want for at least one year, because, in the first place, they will find it much easier to dispose of any surplus they may chance to have, than to procure supplies; in the second place, the cost of the transportation of a year's stock of provisions will be scarcely more than that of a quantity sufficient for two or three months; and, thirdly, one hundred per cent. at least will be saved in the first cost of provisions, if taken from the States.

Families emigrating to Texas should also be well supplied with all kinds of useful furniture, as well to be secure of having them as to save expense in the cost of the articles, for it might be impossible to procure them in Texas at any price. The furniture of the country was very much destroyed in the late invasion, and the great expense of getting it there, has since kept it very scarce.

Above all, families emigrating to Texas should make provision beforehand for a comfortable house, and not suppose, that, because removing, perhaps, to a warmer climate, of the salubrity of which they have heard much, they can "camp out," or they can "get along any way." Many have fallen victims to their improvidence in this respect. Though the climate of Texas *is*, generally, very mild and salubrious, yet there is a rainy season, when the new settler, especially, needs a tight and comfortable dwelling. For three months of the year, too, "Northers," as winds from the North are called, are frequent, and during their prevalence the cold is often severe. The peculiarities of the country, already noticed, which render the summers cool and pleasant, cause two or three of the winter months to be comparatively cold and bleak.

Every individual emigrating to Texas should also be well provided with substantial warm clothing for winter, as well as light clothing for summer. Summer clothing is not a sufficient protection against the Northers peculiar to the country in winter.

As gardens, garden vegetables, and fruits, are generally scarce in Texas, the emigrant should take along a good supply of seeds, and also, if practicable, young peach, apricot, plum, and other trees. Such a precaution will contribute exceedingly to the health, comfort, and pleasure, as well as to the support, of the new settler.

Families will do well to take with them also horses and stock; which, in case of their travelling by land, or by the course of the rivers, will be practicable to some extent.

In respect to lands, of which every emigrant expects to purchase more or less, it may be said, in the general, that as good titles may be had in Texas as in any other country, but that more caution is requisite there to avoid those that are bad, than perhaps any where else. The great number of spurious titles to Texan lands should not discourage the emigrant: it is one of the best proofs he can have of the great excellence and value of those lands; for as men counterfeit the precious, and not common metals, so they eagerly engage in speculations in the most fertile and valuable lands, and not those of a poor or indifferent quality; and it is evident that the spurious land titles in Texas are very much the result of an eager and continuous speculation in those lands for years.

A full exposition of all that relates to Texan land titles might require a year's study and a volume of matter. But such an exposition the emigrant does not want: he wants to ascertain, in the shortest way possible, what titles are unquestionable, what doubtful, and what are esteemed bad.

More particularly, then, in the first place, it may be said, that all titles emanating from the Texan Government are good; but then it behooves the emigrant to know of whom he purchases such, as well as other titles. It may be, there was some illegality in the transfer of a title to the holder; that he is not a citizen of the country; or that he purchased of one whose land had been granted on conditions which forbade him to sell.

Again, secondly, all titles to lands regularly obtained under the Mexican, hold good under the Texan Government, *provided* the holder of the same has not forfeited his land by abandoning the country during the war, or by joining the enemy, or otherwise. But since these titles, no doubt generally of the best kind, may be thus rendered worthless, the emigrant should not place unlimited confidence in them.

Again, the same land may be sold by the same individual more than once; or, owing to mistakes or designed frauds in surveys and locations, there may be different claimants for the same land. Let the emigrant be, then, on his guard.

The writer, however, does not mean to convey the idea that the liability of the new settler in Texas to make bad purchases of land is owing to a greater dishonesty of the people there than elsewhere, but rather to the fact, already mentioned, of an eager and long continued speculation in Texan lands. Many a Texan may hold a spurious title, and believe it to be good.

Though the emigrant to Texas is no longer entitled to bounty land from the Government, yet he may still purchase very excellent located land at from a dollar to three dollars per acre, and claims to lands unlocated at a much lower rate. Such will not be the case long, however. Lands are fast rising in value.

In this connection it may be well to make a few remarks upon Empresario Grants, Texas Land Companies, and their "Scrip." The history of one Company, embracing an account of the grants for the completion of the conditions, or the disposal of which the Company was formed; and also of its scrip, will, it is believed, furnish important information in respect to other Companies.

In 1829, Lorenzo de Zavala, late Governor of the State of Mexico, petitioned the Government of the State of Coahuila and Texas, for permission to introduce into the latter country five hundred families, on the conditions allowed by the Mexican Colonization Laws. The petition was *granted;* also, a petition of Zavala to the Supreme Government, for permission to locate the five hundred families in a portion of the public domain of Texas, which had been "reserved" by that Government, was *granted.* In these grants, by the way, is presented the substance of that which constituted the so-called Empresario *Grants* of Zavala and others. They consisted in a permission to introduce, within certain defined limits in Texas, a certain number of families ; and in a claim, when the families,

16*

or a certain part of them, were settled in Texas, to a certain amount of premium land.

About the time that Zavala obtained his grant, Whelin, an apothecary of the city of Mexico, obtained an adjoining grant, i. e. permission to introduce a certain number of families into a portion of the domain of Texas, adjoining that granted, as now described, to Zavala.

In 1829 or 1830, Zavala, in the city of New-York, met with Judge Burnet, of Texas, who also had a grant. Whereupon they, Zavala and Burnet, sold out their grants—and, by power of attorney, the former that of Whelin also—to a company which they formed, or which was formed, in the city of New-York, for making the purchase.    This sale—though evidently never contemplated by either the Supreme Government or that of Coahuila and Texas, at the time the National and State Colonization Laws were enacted—was probably in good faith on the part of the said Empresarios, Zavala and Burnet: they believing, whether correctly or not, that they had the right to dispose of their grants.    If they *had,* then the said Company, *in case it had introduced the families contracted for by the said Empresarios,* and in the *time specified* in their contracts, would have been entitled to all the profits which would have accrued to the contractors, had they fulfilled their own contracts.    However this may have been—viz. the above-named right of the Empresarios, and, in the case supposed, of the Company—it seems that said Company did *not* fulfil the contracts of the said Empresarios, but first formed a joint stock of their purchase, and then sold out their stock, or a part of it ; whereupon the stockholders issued scrip. This scrip, printed on fine bank note paper, and in an otherwise imposing style, and thus well calculated to secure the confidence of the ignorant and unwary, was sold indiscriminately to all who would purchase, whether with the view of settling in Texas or not. To such purchasers as never settled in Texas, it is evident that the scrip could have been of no use ; because none but *actual settlers* could hold land in Texas, except perhaps by purchase from a *native* Mexican. And, again, to such purchasers of scrip as *did* settle in Texas, it is not easy to see how the scrip could have been of value, because, *as* settlers, they were entitled to bounty lands direct from the Government ; and they could not receive such lands and also avail themselves of their scrip, and thus receive, in effect, a double bounty fron the Government. But, independent of all this, there was a radical error in the transactions of the Company under consideration : their stock and scrip were sold upon the supposition, or *as if*, when they purchased the above described grants, they had actually purchased all the land within the limits of those grants and held the same in fee simple, than which nothing can be more erroneous ; for the grantees themselves, Zavala, Burnet and Whelin, had not a claim to a foot of land within their so-called grants, except in so far as they fulfilled their contracts by the introduction of actual settlers—which settlers must have been families, and to the number of at least one hundred. If they had introduced ninety-nine families, and not the hundredth, they were entitled to no proportion of premium land whatever ; nor for one hundred and ninety-nine families, more than for one hundred.   The result of all is, then, that the scrip issued by the said Company neither is nor was ever worth a stiver.


## EDUCATION.

Since the war, education has been much neglected—the necessary result of the unsettled state of the country, and the want of teachers.  But the people of Texas, like those from whom they sprung, are awake to its importance.  It is one of the great leading objects upon which the man of family keeps his eye, and upon which the Texan statesman forgets not to ponder. Good schools will doubtless very soon and generally be established by the exertions of individuals and neighborhoods.  Some leading men in Congress, and at least one influential member of the present Administration, are disposed to exert themselves to establish a general system of education.  It was expected that a plan would have been presented to Congress during its late session ; but a multiplicity of more pressing business probably prevented.

There are already some few places in Texas which offer flattering prospects to the teacher ; and such will rapidly increase with the progressive settlement of the country.   Indeed, to the well qualified teacher, who, with elevated views, would be extensively useful, and value a reputation in his profession, and a high standing in community, as well as prospective pecuniary profit, Texas generally, and at the present time, offers very encouraging prospects.   Such a teacher, establishing himself in that country now, might lay the foundation of a reputation and usefulness, as well as fortune, which, at a subsequent period, might be impossible.

Parents, who have the means, are now very generally sending their children to the United States to be educated; but there can be no good reason for the continuance of this custom.  More delightful and healthy locations for schools and colleges cannot be found in America, than in Texas; and the expense of living, in the more healthy sections of the country, cannot, eventually, be much, if any, greater than in the Northern and Middle States; for, with the exception perhaps of wheat, all the necessaries of life will be raised in abundance in the Northern and Western parts of Texas.


## MORALS.

There is existing in the minds of the people in many places, if not generally, at the North, a strong and bitter prejudice against Texas.  The writer, in making this assertion, is aware that he is advancing a serious charge against his countrymen; for prejudice is ungenerous, unreasonable, and a very fruitful source of evil.  It is ungenerous, because it is *pre-judging*—judging before evidence—and, what is worse, without seeking, and even often without admitting evidence.  What can be more illiberal, as well as unreasonable?  It is unreasonable, again, because not only founded upon ignorance, but more or less a conscious ignorance.  It is a fruitful source of evil, because it leads to assertions and actions generally unsustained by facts, and totally wrong.

But why this prejudice against Texas?  Because it

has been represented to be the resort of criminals, of insolvent and fraudulent debtors, of outlaws, and bad characters of every description. Now, it cannot be, by any reasonable man, believed that the *majority* of the people of Texas are of such a character ; for, if they were, how could they have achieved their Independence ? and how could they have established a regular and efficient Government,—which, beyond all question, they have ? No : it is believed only that a *large part* of the people of Texas are of the character described. Well, admitting they are, should the entire population and country be then reviled ? Should it not rather be matter of rejoicing to every lover of Liberty, of liberal institutions—to every one desirous of the extension of Christianity and of knowledge—that a portion of the Anglo-American race have planted in the wilderness of the South and West—where despotism and savage cruelty had prevailed—the institutions which were their birth-right ? And should it not be hoped that this race, and these institutions, may be spread over the entire continent of America ? For, certainly, a people like the Texans, however bad many of them may be, who are capable of establishing and sustaining a free Government, and liberal and enlightened institutions, are capable of ameliorating the condition of savages, and of men ignorant, and degraded, and enslaved by despotic Government. But if—admitting that many are of bad character—the entire people of Texas must, therefore, be reviled, why not make the same application of the rule elsewhere ? Why not revile the people of Maryland, of the Carolinas, of Vermont, and of the city of New York ? Maryland and the Carolinas, if the writer has been rightly informed, were at first settled very much by criminals and outlaws. Vermont, not many years ago, was the resort of insolvent, if not of fraudulent debtors ; and New York is, to-day, and constantly, the resort of every species of bad character. By a late report of the Police, it appears that four thousand individuals were presented for trial in the city of New-York in the course of one year. Now, the population of New-York is, we will say, three times that of Texas ; but not a third, no, nor an eighth part, of four thousand individuals, have, in the same time, been presented for trial in Texas ; and offenders against the law do not now more escape trial in that country, than in any other, as new and thinly settled. Indeed, if, in the proportion of the entire population of Texas to that of the city of New York, there were as many criminals and other bad characters in the former as in the latter, it would be impossible to live in Texas with any thing like security of person or property, because of its extent of territory and scattered population.

But it is not admitted, nor the fact, that a large portion of the people of Texas are of the character above described. According to the best information which the author was able to obtain, whilst in Texas, in respect to the morals of the people, down to the commencement of the war in 1835, there could not be found in any of the United States of the North, a people more generally honest, honorable, hospitable, kind and peaceable, than were the people of Texas. Bankrupts and outlaws from the United States, had, to be sure, settled among them, and particularly along the boundary of the two countries ; but they had not corrupted the community, nor caused special disturbance. Since the war, it must be confessed, that in some of the sea-board and other more accessible and important towns—which have been the resort of the refuse soldiery of the country, and of loose and abandoned characters from the South and West of the States—the society has been decidedly bad. But, even in these places, the morals of the people are rapidly improving. Having now laws for the punishment of immorality and crime, and aware of the character which they have generally, though unjustly, sustained in the United States, the people of Texas seem resolved that their laws shall be rigidly executed.

It is worthy of special remark, as an earnest of the future execution of the laws in Texas, that a judge of one of the higher courts has lately, in his entire circuit, beginning at the city of Houston, condemned all criminals presented for trial; and that in this decided and rigid course of administration of justice, he has not only been sustained, but applauded. So far, then, justice in Texas has had " free course, run, and" been " glorified."

## RELIGION.

At first, under the Spanish Government, the only religion tolerated in Texas was the Roman Catholic; and though subsequently, under the Mexican Government, the Protestant religion was tolerated previous to the Revolution, yet it had made but little progress. Since that event, religious toleration is the same in Texas as in the United States. As yet, however, not much has been done for the religious improvement of the people.

Though, on the one hand, the people of Texas, with few exceptions, may be apparently little anxious for the establishment among them of the institutions of Christianity ; yet, on the other, they are far from being generally Atheists and scoffers at religion. Having been perhaps generally raised in those parts of the United States where religious instruction was comparatively little known and valued, and having lived a considerable time in Texas with scarcely any religious privileges at all, many of the Texans value churches and ministers of religion, if not religion itself, less than otherwise they would. And yet the erection of a church in a rising village is by no means a matter overlooked ; and the people intend, by and by, at least, when it shall be more convenient, not only to have churches, but clergymen to officiate in them. The Government, too, has not failed, in some degree, to show its respect for Christianity. From the Executive down to the Representative in Congress, the same devout acknowledgment of a kind, superintending Providence, is wont to be expressed, as is common on the part of those in like stations in the United States.

The Author is not aware of the erection, as yet, of more than one Protestant Church in Texas, at San Augustine. The citizens of Matagorda have obtained a charter for an Episcopal Church, and will doubtless soon have one erected. In other places, subscriptions have been started, and other incipient steps taken, towards the erection of Churches.

That which the Author has remarked more than any thing else, to the credit of the Texans, in respect of religion, is, their disposition to attend upon the preach-

17

ing of the Gospel when opportunity offers, and their marked attention and respectful deportment in attendance. No laughing nor sneering, nor unnecessary noise, is to be observed in, or in the neighborhood of, a place of worship. Such conduct Texans consider beneath them, and will not countenance.

For these reasons, the pious clergyman might labor with more satisfaction and hope of success, in Texas, than in many parts of the United States. Indeed, Texas is an inviting field for the devoted and pious clergymen of different denominations; and God grant that many such may speedily go there, that future generations in that country, like the people of New-England, may grow up with the impression that the institutions of Christianity are their heritage and birth-right, and that they must be supported.

# APPENDIX.

---

No. 1.—*Capture of Santa Anna, &c.*

The following account of the capture of Santa Anna, on the 22d of April, 1836, the day after the battle of San Jacinto, is given on the authority of an officer present at that battle :

On the morning of the 22d of April the report came into camp that Messrs. Carnes and Secretts, with about twenty or twenty-five soldiers, had hemmed in Santa Anna and Cos, with about fifty Mexicans, ten miles from camp. Col. Burleson came round for volunteers to accompany him as a reinforcement. He soon raised fifty or fifty-five mounted men, and they proceeded to Sim's Bayou, near Vince's, where they expected to join Carnes' party ; but, not being able to overtake them, hesitated whether to follow them on to the Brazos—where it was understood they had gone— or to return to the camp. Finally, thirty of the party agreed to go on : the balance made a move to return to the camp. When they arrived at Vince's, it was proposed to go down Buffalo Bayou, which was accordingly done. They had positive orders from Burleson not to kill any prisoners, but to bring them into camp. They had not proceeded far, when they espied some four or five deer on the west side of a branch that made into the prairie from the Bayou. They rode on within forty or fifty yards of the branch, when they halted. The deer started, and, on looking to the right, they espied a Mexican, bending his course towards the bridge : he stopped a moment to gaze around him, and then started on. They rode up to where he was. As soon as he saw them, he laid down in the grass, which was high enough to hide him from their view. When they arrived at the 'spot, he was lying on his side, with a blanket over his face. They called to him to rise, when he only took the blanket from his face. They called to him a second time, and a third, to get up; whereupon he rose and stood up for a moment, and, finding himself surrounded, advanced towards them and desired to shake hands; whereupon one immediately offered him his hand. He pressed and kissed it. He then offered them, as a bribe, a splendid watch, exceedingly valuable jewelry, and a large sum of money, which, to their great credit, and to the credit of the American as well as Texan character, they refused. He then asked where their brave Houston was. They replied he was in camp. Through one of the party, acting as interpreter, they asked him who he was. He replied a private soldier; when one observing the bosom of his shirt, which was very splendid, directed his attention to it. He immediately said that he was an aid to Santa Anna, and burst into a flood of tears. He was told in a mild tone not to grieve, he should not be hurt. He was dressed in common clothes, had no arms, and appeared dejected, complaining of pains in the breast and legs, and of not being able to walk. They proceeded with him two or three miles, which distance he rode. He then dismounted, and walked into camp, where he was conducted by Messrs. Miles, Thompson, and Vermillion.

When conducted into the tent of Gen. Houston, Santa Anna addressed him as follows :—" Soy Antonio Lopez de Santa Anna, Presidente de la Republica Mexicana, y General-en-Gefe del Egerito de Operaciones."

The following account relative to Santa Anna, immediately subsequent to his capture, is as substantially related to the author by Gen. Houston :—

The General was lying upon a blanket at the root of a tree, with his saddle for a pillow, when Santa Anna approached his tent, studiously inquiring for *Houston*. The General was in a partial slumber, and lying, for the sake of an easy position for his wounded ancle, upon his left side, with his face turned from Santa Anna as he approached. The first he knew of Santa Anna's presence was by a squeeze of the hand, and the calling of his name ; whereupon he looked upon Santa Anna with a mild expression of countenance, which seemed to inspire him with confidence and hope of life, which he had evidently expected to forfeit. The General desired him to be seated upon a medicine chest standing by, upon which accordingly he sat down, much agitated, with his hands pressed against his chest. Presently he asked for opium, which being given him, he swallowed a considerable quantity, and soon became more composed. He said to Gen. Houston—" You were born to no ordinary destiny ; you have conquered the Napoleon of the West." He soon desired to know what disposal was to be made of him ; whereupon Gen. Houston, waiving the question, told him he must order all the Mexican troops in Texas to march beyond the Rio Grande, and then spoke of his late cruelty to the Texans, and first at the Alamo ; upon which Santa Anna said, that at the Alamo he had acted according to the laws of war of all nations. The General then spoke of the massacre of Fannin and his men, and said to Santa Anna, " You cannot be so exculpable in that deed, for Fannin surrendered upon capitulation ;" upon which Santa Anna denied that any treaty had been made with Fannin, and proceeded to say that the execution of Fannin and his men was in obedience to the orders of the Mexican Government. " You are that Government, and it has been represented that a treaty *was* made with Fannin," said Gen. Houston ; and then remarked, that, any way, even had the massacre at Goliad been ordered by the Government of Mexico, it was of a nature not to be justified by modern usages of war, and that in disobeying such an order, he would have shown himself a magnanimous commander, and would have been justified by the world ; whereupon Santa Anna remarked that the Mexican Government could not consider Americans in Texas as in any sense a nation ; that they had not even been fighting under a Revolutionary standard, and could only be considered as banditti or land pirates. Upon this the subject of conversation was waived, and, it being night, the General asked Santa Anna if he would have his camp bed, which, being desired, the General ordered it to be brought into his tent. Santa Anna reclined upon it, but did not sleep during the night, being in constant dread of assassination. A majority of the Texans in camp were anxious for his execution ; and, had it not been for the firmness of Gen. Houston, his life would immediately have appeased the just vengeance of his enemies.

\*       \*       \*       \*       \*       \*       \*

It is the opinion of Gen. Houston that Santa Anna is one of the ablest men of the age, and that he sustained himself after his capture as well as any man in like circumstances could. It is the opinion of other Texans that Santa Anna exhibited great address and knowledge of human nature whilst a prisoner, and that, indeed, they never met with a more talented man.

Gen. Houston with difficulty preserved the life of Santa Anna, and with still greater difficulty effected his liberation, which he did in the firm conviction that it would result in good to Texas. He believed that to keep Santa Anna a prisoner would only be a useless expense, but that, if sent back to Mexico, his presence would be at least a constant check upon the Government in any movement it might make to effect another invasion of Texas, because, besides Bustamente, he was the only sufficiently popular man to command a strong party in Mexico, and that Bustamente could never, with safety to himself, lead or send an army into Texas whilst Santa Anna was in Mexico. Santa Anna himself, if reinstated in power, would not, Gen. Houston believed, lead another army into Texas, because he was evidently too well convinced of the great uncertainty of success to try the experiment again ; and he would not, the General believed furthermore, confer the command of an army, destined to operate against Texas, upon another, lest his own glory should be yet more eclipsed in a more successful rival.  \*       \*       \*       \*       \*       \*       \*       \*

The blade of the sword which Santa Anna wore in the battle of

17\*

San Jacinto, was found stuck in the ground; the hilt, valued at $7000, had been broken off by some one who had been careful to secure and secrete so valuable a prize.

Santa Anna, it is said, wore in his shirt three studs, valued at $1700 each; upon these was written his name, in parts, as follows: *Antonio—Lopez de—Santa Anna.* His camp furniture was exceedingly rich and splendid; he had silver tea urns, silver cream pots; splendid china ware, marked in monograms; rich cut glass tumblers and decanters, the latter with stoppers mounted with gold; and almost every thing compatible with a camp which could contribute to comfort and luxury.

### No. 2.—*Exposition made by the Ayuntamiento and Inhabitants of Austin's Colony, explanatory of the late commotions, and ad_hering to the plan of Santa Anna. Adopted July 27th,* 1832.

The causes of the late disturbances are plain to every person who resides in Texas, or is informed of the events which have transpired here since the commencement of the year 1830; but as those causes have never been laid before the Mexican people, it is necessary and proper that it should now be done, as a justification of the course taken by a large and respectable portion of the inhabitants, and also as explanatory of the reasons which have impelled the Ayuntamiento and the inhabitants of this Colony unanimously to adhere to the plan of Vera Cruz.

From the time when a national and state law invited persons of all nations to come and settle in the wilderness of Texas, *duties* and *rights* were established between those who govern and those who were to obey in virtue of them. Those laws and the general and state constitutions have clearly designated the guarantees which secure the citizens from the caprice and the arbitrary will of the subaltern authorities. But, unfortunately, since the present Administration went into power, an uninterrupted series of depredations, calumnies and injustice, has been the recompense received by the citizens of Texas, for their firm adhesion to the Mexican Republic and to the Federal system by which it is governed. The civil authorities have been viewed by the military as mere subalterns, to be commanded as a corporal commands a so'dier. This military power, under the authority of the superior chief, has disregarded all the rights which the constitution secures to free citizens, and has wished to subject every thing to its enslaving influence. The Government of the State of Coahuila and Texas has not exercised in these Colonies any more power than what the superior military chief has been pleased to grant as a favor.

To enumerate in detail all the violations of the constitution and laws, and attacks upon the rights of the State of Coahuila and Texas, which have been committed by the military authority, would occupy more time and space than the present occasion will admit; only a few of the leading ones will, therefore, be mentioned, which have had a direct influence in producing the late disturbances.

First—On the 22d April, 1828, concessions of land were made in conformity with the colonization laws by the President of the nation, Don Guadalupe Victoria, and the Governor of this State, to the inhabitants established East of the San Jacinto, and in the district of Nacogdoches. In the year 1830, Don Francisco Madero was appointed by the Governor a Commissioner to survey the said land, and issue the titles in due form of law to said settlers. He arrived on the Trinity river in the month of January, 1831, and had made some progress in the discharge of his duties, when he and his surveyor, Jose Maria Carbajal, were arrested by Col. Juan Davis Bradburn, Military Commandant of Anahuac, and conducted to that post as prisoners. The only reason given by said Commandant for this direct and insulting attack upon the constitution and sovereignty of the State of Coahuila and Texas, was, that the arrest of Madero was in obedience to the orders of his Excellency the Commandant, Gen. Don Manuel de Mier y Teran. Similar orders were issued for the arrest of Madero to Col. Don Jose de las Peidras, Commandant of the frontier at Nacogdoches. His Excellency the Governor of the State speaks of this affair in his message to the Legislature, at the opening of the session on the 21 January last, in the following words, as translated:

" The public tranquillity has not been disturbed in any part of the State, although Col. Davis Bradburn assumed the power without the knowledge of this Government, to arrest a commissioner appointed by it to survey vacant lands and issue titles,—which act might have caused a commotion; but nothing of the kind occurred, owing to the prudence of the arrested person, and of the citizens who were to have received titles for lands, and who, by this event, were deprived for the time being from obtaining legal possession of their property. This Government endeavored to ascertain the cause of this interference, and for that purpose entered into continued communications with the Commandant General of the States, and so learned, that said General thinks that, agreeably to the commission conferred upon him by the Supreme Government of the Union, under the third article of the national law of 6th April, 1830, the commission of said arrested commissioner was in opposition to the 11th article of said general law; and notwithstanding he has been assured that such is not the case, he still persists in his opinion. For these reasons, this matter is in such a situation, that, to remove the obstacles, it would be necessary to adopt measures that *might compromit the State to the highest degree.*"

Second—On the 10th December last, the Commandant General, by a laconic military order, annulled the Ayuntamiento of Liberty, which was legally established by the commissioner Madero, and established a new Ayuntamiento at Anahuac, without any authority from the State Government, and without even consulting it.

Third—The Commandant General has, without any authority from the State, taken possession of, and appropriated, such lands as he deemed proper; thus totally disregarding the rights and sovereignty of the State. Speaking of this subject, the Governor, in the before-mentioned message, says (as translated,) "Although this Government, in the message of last year, expressed a hope, that under the provisions of the law of 6th April, 1830, a considerable colonization of the vacant lands in the department of Bexar might be expected, nothing has been done up to the present time. The commissioner of the General Government, notwithstanding the instructions he has received, to purchase from the State a portion of vacant lands, has not entered into the necessary contracts for this purpose, nor made any proposition to do so; but has, without any authority, occupied many points with garrisons. This Government is ignorant of the causes of this strange mode of proceeding, and therefore cannot state what they are."

Fourth—The Government of the State ordered U. B. Johnston, the Alcalde of Liberty, to convene the people, and hold an election for Alcalde and members of the Ayuntamiento of Liberty, notwithstanding the order of Gen. Teran, before cited, annulling that corporation. Col. Bradburn issued orders, and repeated and reiterated them, to said Johnston, prohibiting him from proceeding with said election, and threatening him with military force; in consequence of which, the election was not held, and thus the order of the State Government was disregarded by the military power, and the citizens were by military force prevented from exercising the rights of suffrage which the constitution and laws guaranteed to them.

Fifth—Col. Bradburn has, at various times, and without any regard whatever to the constitution or the authorities of the State of Coahuila and Texas, arrested peaceable and quiet citizens, for no other reason than an expression of opinion against his violent and arbitrary acts; and he has disregarded the rights of persons and of property, which were expressly guaranteed by the National and State constitutions, and attempted to make every thing bend to military despotism and martial law. Encouraged by the patience of the State Government, under the iron rod of military power, his despotism reached its highest point. In the month of May last, he imprisoned seven citizens, and attempted to arrest George M. Patrick, the first Regidor, and acting Alcalde of Anahuac, and James Lindsey, another Regidor of the Ayuntamiento of that place, who, in consequence, left Anahuac, and fled to Austin's Colony for security.

These repeated and continued acts of despotism, added to the highly abusive manner in which Col. Bradburn expressed himself against
the citizens, and his threats against the constitutional authorities
of the State, finally exhausted the patience of all, and caused an
excitement which spread through every part of the country. The
quiet and peaceable citizens had looked on in silence, with their
eyes and hopes directed to the State Government, as the only constitutional authority competent to rem dy evils of such magnitude,
but, unfortunately, the State Government was then borne down by
the same iron rod that was held over Texas. His Excellency the
Governor, in his message before quoted, very plainly says that he
cannot sustain the constitution and laws of the State against military encroachments, without *compromitting the public tranquillity in the highest degree*—which is saying, in substance, that a
resistance by force was the only alternative left to him, and this he
was not authorized to adopt, without the previous sanction of the
Legislature. His Excellency, therefore, did all he could without
an open declaration of war against the military.

In this state of things, the citizens, goaded to desperation by
military despotism on the one hand, and seeing, on the other, that
the State Government had in vain made every effort of a pacific
nature to sustain itself, and protect them, considered that petitions
made on paper were useless—that they would in fact only have
given new opportunities to the military to ridicule and trample
upon the State authorities, and to rivet their chains more firmly.

The last and only remedy left to an oppressed people was then
resorted to, and, without any previous combination or organized
plans, a large number of citizens, moved by a common and simul-
taneous influence, took up arms, and marched to Anahuac, to release the prisoners whom Bradburn had illegally confined, to re-
establish the Ayuntamiento of Liberty, and to prove to him that
the authorities of the State of Coahuila and Texas could not any
longer be trampled upon with impunity by the military power.
Such were the causes, and the only ones, which produced the attack upon Juan Davis Bradburn, at the military post of Anahuac.

Nothstanding the efforts of the administration of Bustamente
to conceal the situation of things, the people by this time had
learned that the exercise of military despotism was not confined to
Texas, but that the whole Republic was governed by the same iron
sceptre ; that the same causes which had disturbed the public
tranquillity here, had roused the spirit of the free and enlightened
Mexicans in every part of this great confederation ; and that, on the
2d January last, the heroic city of Vera Cruz had pronounced in
favor of the constitution and laws, headed by the distinguished
patriot Gen. Don Antonio Lopez de Santa Anna ; and being convinced that the last hope of Liberty, and the principles of the representative Democratic Federal system, depended on the success
of the Liberal Party, of which Santa Anna was the leader, the citi-

zens who were under arms against Bradburn, at the Camp on Turtle Bayou, near Anahuac, on the 13th of June, unanimously adhered to the plan of Vera Cruz, by adopting the following resolutions :

" Resolved, That we view with feelings of the deepest regret, the manner in which the Government of the Republic of Mexico is administered by the present dynasty. The repeated violations of the constitution ; the total disregard of the law ; the entire prostration of the civil authority, and the substitution in its stead of a military despotism, are grievances of such a character as to arouse the feelings of every fr· eman, and impel him to resistance.

" Resolved, That we view with feelings of the deepest interest and solicitude the firm and manly resistance which is made by the highly talented and distinguished chieftain, Gen. Santa Anna, to the numberless encroachments and infractions which have been made by the present Administration upon the constitution and laws of our adopted and beloved country.

" Resolved, That, as *freemen*, devoted to a correct interpretation and enforcement of the constitution and laws, according to their true spirit, we pledge our lives and fortunes in support of the same, and of the distinguished leader who is now so gallantly fighting in defence of civil liberty.

" Resolved, That the people of Texas be invited to co-operate with us in support of the principles incorporated in the foregoing resolutions."

The citizens of Brazoria, and of the precinct of Victoria in this Colony, also pronounced in favor of said plan. A deputation was sent to Lieutenant Colonel Ugartecha, the commandant of Velasco, inviting him to adhere to said plan, which he refused. This left those who had pronounced no alternative but to attack him : they did so on the 27th June, under the command of the 2d Alcalde of this Jurisdiction, John Austin ; and after a bloody battle, in which the most determined bravery was displayed on both sides, the fort surrendered to the *Santa Anna Forces*, and not to a faction of rebels against the nation, as had been erroneously stated by the enemies of Texas and of its inhabitants.

The Ayuntamiento of the Jurisdiction of Austin were impressed with the importance of preserving the public tranquillity, and felt the peculiarly delicate situation of the settlers of those Colonies, owing to their being of foreign birth. It was well known that every species of calumny had been heaped upon them by the enemies of Texas, and of a republican and enlightened emigration, with the design of reviving amongst the Mexicans the old Spanish prejudices against persons born in another country. It was feared that those enemies would take advantage of any disturbances here to pervert the truth, and attribute to them hostile views against the Mexican territory and Federal Constitution. This body was under the immediate eye and direction of the Political Chief of the De-

partment, who was then in this town, and equally anxious to preserve the public tranquillity ; and who, we are assured, is as much
opposed to military encroachments as any other man in the community. It will also be remembered that the Ayuntamiento had
no means of acquiring information as to the true state of things in
the interior of this Republic, the only newspaper that was permitted to reach here through the Post-Office Department was the Min-
isterial " Registro Official." Under these circumstances, this body
used every effort to preserve good order and keep the settlers from
participating in the present civil war ; and it is probable that these
efforts would have been successful, had not events been precipitated
in the manner they have been by the tyrannical and illegal acts of
Col. Bradburn. But now, as public opinion has expressed itself
in the most decided and unequivocal manner, in favor of the plan
of Vera Cruz, the same reasons which prevented the Ayuntamiento
from taking an early lead in this question, have impelled that body
to unite with the people in adhering to said plan ; which reasons
are, the preservation of harmony, and the advancement of the general good, which can alone be effected by the most perfect union.

## No. 3. —*Extract from the Petition of the People of Texas to the General Congress of the United Mexican States.*

Our misfortunes pervade the whole territory—operate upon the
whole population ; and are as diversified in character, as our public interests and necessities are various. Texas, at large, feels and
deplores an utter destitution of the common benefits which have
usually accrued from the worst system of internal government,
that the patience of mankind ever tolerated. She is virtually
without a *government*—and if she is not precipitated into all the
unspeakable horrors of anarchy, it is only because there is a re-
deeming spirit among the people, which still infuses a moral en-
ergy into the miserable fragments of authority that exist among
us. We are perfectly sensible that a large portion of our population, usually denominated " the Colonists," and composed of An-
glo-Americans, have been greatly calumniated before the Mexican
Government. But could the honorable Congress scrutinize strict-
ly into our real condition ; could they see and understand the
wretched confusion in all the elements of Government which we
daily feel and deplore ; our ears would no longer be insulted, nor
our feelings mortified, by the artful fictions of hireling emissaries
from abroad, nor by the malignant aspersions of disappointed military commandants at home.

Our grievances do not so much result from any positive misfea-
sance on the part of the present State Authorities, as from the total

absence, or the very feeble and mutile dispensation of those restrictive influences, which it is the appropriate design of the social compact to exercise upon the people, and which are necessary to fulfil the ends of civil society. We complain more of the *want* of *all* the important attributes of government, than of the abuses of any. &ast; &ast; &ast; &ast; &ast; &ast; &ast; &ast;

But, independent of these general truths, there are some impressive reasons why the peace and happiness of Texas demand a local Government. Constituting a remote frontier of the Republic, and bordering on a powerful nation, a portion of whose population, in juxta-position to hers, is notoriously profligate and lawless, she requires, in a peculiar and emphatic sense, the vigorous application of such laws as are necessary, not only to the preservation of good order, the protection of property, and the redress of personal wrongs, but such, also, as are essential to the prevention of illicit commerce, to the security of the public revenues, and to the avoidance of serious collision with the authorities of the neighboring Republic. That such a judicial administration is impracticable under the present arrangement, is too forcibly illustrated by the past, to admit of any rational hope for the future.

It is an acknowledged principle in the science of jurisprudence, that the prompt and certain infliction of mild and humane punishments is more efficacious for the prevention of crime, than a tardy and precarious administration of the most sanguinary penal code. Texas is virtually denied the benefit of this benevolent rule, by the locality and the character of her present Government. Crimes of the greatest atrocity may go unpunished, and hardened criminals triumph in their iniquity, because of the difficulties and delays which encumber her judicial system, and necessarily intervene a trial and a conviction, and the sentence and the execution of the law. Our " Supreme Tribunal of Justice" holds its sessions upwards of seven hundred miles distant from our central population ; and that distance is greatly enlarged, and sometimes made impassable, by the casualties incident to a *mail* conducted by a single horseman through a wilderness, often infested by vagrant and murderous Indians. Before sentence can be pronounced by the local courts on persons charged with the most atrocious crimes, the copy of the process must be transmitted to an asesor, resident at Leona Vicario, who is too far removed from the scene of guilt to appreciate the importance of a speedy decision, and is too much estranged from our civil and domestic concerns, to feel the miseries that result from a total want of legal protection in person and property. But our difficulties do not terminate here : After the asesor shall have found leisure to render his opinion, and final judgment is pronounced, it again becomes necessary to resort to the Capital, to submit the tardy sentence to the Supreme Tribunal, for " approbation, revocation, or modification," before the judgment of the law can be executed. Here we have again to encounter the vexations and delays incident to all Governments, where those who exercise its most interesting functions are removed by distance from the people on whom they operate, and for whose benefit the social compact is created.

These repeated delays, resulting from the remoteness of our courts of judicature, are pernicious in many respects : they involve heavy expenses, which, in civil suits, are excessively onerous to litigants, and give to the rich and influential such manifold advantages over the poor, as operate to an absolute exclusion of the latter from the remedial and protective benefits of the law. They offer seductive opportunities and incitements to bribery and corruption, and endanger the sacred purity of the judiciary, which, of all the branches of Government, is most intimately associated with the domestic and social happiness of man, and should therefore be, not only sound and pure, but unsuspected of the venal infection. They present insuperable difficulties to the exercise of the corrective right of recusation, and virtually nullify the constitutional power of impeachment. In criminal actions they are no less injurious. They are equivalent to a license to iniquity, and exert a dangerous influence on the moral feelings at large. Before the tedious process of the law can be complied with, and the criminal, whose hands are perhaps imbrued in a brother's blood, be made to feel its restrictive justice, the remembrance of his crime is partially effaced from the public mind, and the righteous arbitrament of the law, which, if promptly executed, would have received universal approbation, and been a salutary warning to evil-doers, is impugned as vindictive and cruel. The popular feeling is changed from a just indignation of the crime, into an amiable, but mistaken sympathy for the criminal ; and, by an easy and natural transition, is converted into disgust and disaffection towards the Government and its laws.

## No. 4.

The following is one of many documents of like character which might be presented to the public, showing the popular sentiment in Texas, in regard to the Mexican Government, in the summer of 1835 :

MUNICIPALITY OF MINA, July 4th, 1835.

At a General Meeting of the citizens of this Municipality, convened agreeably to public notice, for the purpose of considering the present situation of the relations of Texas with the Government of the Mexican United States, and the purposes connected with the general safety of the country, Dr. Thomas J. Gazley was

18

called to the Chair, and John Moody appointed Secretary. The object of the meeting being explained, the following resolutions were adopted :—

Resolved, That *the People* have entire confidence in the Committee of Safety, and that *all* their acts have the full approbation of this meeting ; and that said Committee be continued, with all its powers.

Resolved, That we feel an entire confidence in the Constitution and Laws of our adopted country, and will at all times sustain the legal authorities in the exercise of their constitutional duties.

Resolved, That Thomas J. Gazley, D. C. Barrett, and Henry P. Hill, be a Committee to draft a Circular to the Ayuntamiento of each Municipality in the Department of Brazos upon the objects contemplated by this meeting, and that the same be submitted to the Committee of Safety for their approbation.

Resolved, That the proceedings of this meeting be signed by the Chairman and Secretary.

THOMAS J. GAZLEY, Chairman.<br>JOHN MOODY, Secretary.

—

Mina, July 9th, 1835.

Gentlemen—On the 4th inst. the citizens of this Municipality met, according to previous appointment, to consult together as to the degree of credence that they should place in the almost numberless reports that have been circulated among them, and the best method of avoiding the cloud of difficulties that seemed hanging over them.

After the maturest deliberation, they came to the conclusion that there was certainly *some* reason to expect a movement of the Government forces towards the Colonies ; and the greatest difficulty was to divine the precise object and intention of that advance.

But they are aware that it would be the blindest credulity to believe, to its full extent, the idle exaggerations that for some time past have agitated the public mind. They forbear to express any opinion whatever as to the *immediate* cause that wrought the present excitements, but deplore the evils that may result from the scisms which have taken place in consequence, and they feel, and deeply feel, the necessity that there is for the existence of some medium through which public opinion can be ascertained and wielded with effect against the irregularities of those whose disregard to the laws of the country has destroyed the mutual confidence, as well as mutual respect, between them and their fellow-citizens of the Mexican Republic, inasmuch as the misconduct of a *few designing men* is attributed to the *whole* community, and construed into disaffection to the General Government.

They are by no means of opinion, while making their own feelings their standard, that the whole of Texas, generally, cherish a hostile disposition to Mexicans or the Mexican Government, when administered on its constitutional principles.

They are voluntary citizens of the same Republic; have sworn to support the same Constitution; and are, by inclination and interest, as well as the most solemn obligation, bound to cherish and sustain the liberal and free institutions of this Republic.

In the present confused state of things, they can devise no better mode of meeting the exigencies of the times, than by an *assemblage of delegates from each Municipality*, at San Felippe, or some other central place, whose duty it shall be to act in council for the people, and in concert with the Executive power still existing in Texas, in providing for the general welfare of a misrepresented, but a determined people.

To effect which object, this meeting appointed a Committee of Address, with instructions to submit its views to the Committee of Safety, for revisal and approbation; and that the said Committee should send a copy to the Ayuntamiento of each Municipality in the Department of Brazos, requesting their co-operation in the plan of sending delegates, as we have before suggested, and their union in the common objects of safety and general defence of our constitutional rights.

HENRY P. HILL,

THOMAS J. GAZLEY,

*Committee of Address.*

No. 5.—*Inventory of Military Stores delivered in conformity with the Capitulation entered into on the 11th of December, 1835, between General Martin Perfecto de Cos, of the Permanent Troops, and General Edward Burleson, of the Colonial Troops of Texas.*

### IN BEXAR.

30 useless muskets, 5 boxes ammunition, 4 drums, 4 boxes with 66 hats and 49 blankets of the company of Lancers, 1 bale with 12 dozen blankets, 1 four-pound cannon, mounted, 1 chinesco, 2 trumpets, 2 clarions, 1 large clarion, 2 cymbals.

### IN THE ALAMO.

2 four-pound cannon, mounted, 1 small brass do., 1 four-pound field-piece, 1 do. three-pounder, complete, 1 rammer, 1 cannon, four-

pounder, with carriage and rammer, 1 iron culverine, of nine-inch calibre, mounted, 1 howitzer of five-inch calibre, 1 cannon, six pounder, 1 field-piece, four-pounder, 1 cannon, three-pounder, mounted, 1 ditto six-pounder, mounted, 257 carabines and muskets.

### IN THE ARSENAL.

11,000 musket cartridges, 2 cartouch boxes, 10 bags grape shot, 9 do. with cartridges, 18 swivel worms, 8 howitzer do., 100 small cannon cartridges, 18 packages musket cartridges, 10 port-fires, 16 swivel worms, 40 swivel cartridges, 1 bag containing 100 pounds of powder, 50 packages cartridges, 16 do. do., 1 box cartridges, damp, 1 box musket cartridges, 1 box powder, 1200 musket cartridges, 1 ammunition box with 20 cannon balls, 10 quick matches, 1 box howitzer worms, 3 boxes musket cartridges, 2 ammunition boxes with 40 cannon balls, 1 match cord, 1 box howitzer worms, 1 box cartridges, 2 do. do., 7 empty ammunition chests, 17 muskets, 1 bugle, 2 boxes ammunition, 1 rammer, 1 lanthorn, 4 large cannon, 2 swivels, 1 four-pound cannon, mounted, 1 box (26 stands) of grape, 1 box musket cartridges, 1 bag of powder, 1 bag of gun flints, 1 drum, 15 carabines, out of order, 11 packages cannon ball, 1 piece small ordnance.

### DELIVERED BY MANCHACA.

67 muskets, 15 coats, 9 gun locks, 49 duck jackets, 1 bunch of wire, 3 bars of steel, 1 small do. of iron, 1 bunch flax thread, 15 skeins sewing silk, 63 duck jackets, 2 barrels containing 166 bayonets, 9 aparejos, 58 lances, 1 pair scales with weights, 1 piece of linsey, 50 muskets with bayonets, 13 lances.

*Bexar, December* 13, 1835.

Delivered by

JUAN CORTINA,
J. FRANCISCO DE RADA,
FRANCISCO HERRERA.

Received by

JAMES CHESHIRE,
WILLIAM G. COOK,
W. H. PATTON.

[Copy.]

F. W. JOHNSON,
*Colonel Commanding.*

No. 6.—*Proclamation of Samuel Houston, Commander-in-Chief of the Army of Texas.*

HEAD QUARTERS, Washington, Dec. 12, 1835.

CITIZENS OF TEXAS—Your situation is peculiarly calculated to call forth all your manly energies. Under the Republican Constitution of Mexico, you were invited to Texas, then a wilderness. You have reclaimed and rendered it a cultivated country. You solemnly swore to support the Constitution and its laws. Your oaths are yet inviolate. In accordance with them, you have fought with the Liberals against those who sought to overthrow the Constitution in 1832, when the present usurper was the champion of Liberal principles in Mexico. Your obedience has manifested your integrity. You have witnessed with pain the convulsions of the interior, and a succession of usurpations. You have experienced in silent grief the expulsion of your members elect from the State Congress. You have realized the horrors of anarchy, and the dictation of military rule. The promises made to you have not been fulfilled. Your memorials for redress of grievances have been disregarded; and the agents you have sent to Mexico have been imprisoned for years, without enjoying the rights of trial according to law. Your constitutional Executive has been deposed by the bayonets of a mercenary soldiery, while your Congress has been dissolved by violence, and its members either fled or were arrested by the military force of the country. The Federation has been dissolved—the Constitution declared at an end, and Centralism has been established. Amidst all these trying vicissitudes you remained loyal to the duty of citizens, with a hope that Liberty would not perish in the Republic of Mexico. But while you were fondly cherishing this hope, the Dictator required the surrender of the arms of the civic militia, that he might be enabled to establish, on the ruins of the Constitution, a system of policy which would forever enslave the people of Mexico. Zakatecas, unwilling to yield her sovereign rights to the demand, which struck at the root of all liberty, refused to disarm her citizens of their private arms. Ill-fated State! her power, as well as her wealth, aroused the ambition of Santa Anna, and excited his cupidity. Her citizens became the first victims of his cruelty, while her wealth was sacrificed in payment for the butchery of her citizens. The success of the usurper determined him in exacting from the people of Texas submission to the Central form of Government; and, to enforce his plan of despotism, he despatched a military force to invade the Colonies, and exact the arms of the inhabitants. The citizens refused the demand, and the invading force was increased. The question then was, shall we resist oppression and live free, or violate our oaths, and wear a despot's stripes? The citizens of

18*

Texas rallied to the defence of their constitutional rights. They have met four to one, and, by their chivalry and courage, they have vanquished the enemy with a gallantry and spirit which is characteristic of the justice of our cause.

The Army of the People is now before Bexar, besieging the Central army within its walls. Though called together at a moment, the citizens of Texas, unprovided as they were in the necessary munitions of war and supplies for an army, have maintained a siege for months. Always patient and untiring in their patriotism and zeal in the cause of Liberty, they have borne every vicissitude of season, and every incident of the soldier, with a contempt of peril which reflects immortal honor on the members of the Army of the People. *     *     *     *     *     *

Citizens of Texas—Your rights must be defended. The oppressors must be driven from our soil. Submission to the laws, and union among ourselves, will render us invincible; subordination and discipline in our army will guarantee to us victory and renown. Our invader has sworn to exterminate us, or sweep us from the soil of Texas. He is vigilant in his work of oppression, and has ordered to Texas ten thousand men to enforce the unhallowed purposes of his ambition. His letters to his subalterns in Texas have been intercepted, and his plans for our destruction are disclosed. Departing from the chivalric principles of civilized warfare, he has ordered arms to be distributed to *a portion of our population*, for the purpose of creating in the midst of us a *servile war*. The hopes of the usurper were inspired by a belief that the people of Texas were disunited and divided in opinion; and that alone has been the cause of the present invasion of our rights. He shall realize the fallacy of his hopes in the union of her citizens, and their ETERNAL RESISTANCE to his plans against constitutional liberty. We will enjoy our birth-right, or *perish in its defence!*

The services of five thousand volunteers will be accepted. By the first of March next we must meet the enemy with an army worthy of our cause, and which will reflect honor upon freemen. Our habitations must be defended; the sanctity of our hearths and firesides must be defended from pollution. Liberal Mexicans will unite with us; our countrymen in the field have presented an example worthy of imitation. Generous and brave hearts from a land of Freedom have joined our standard before Bexar. They have, by their heroism and valor, called forth the admiration of their comrades in arms, and have reflected additional honor on the land of their birth.

Let the brave rally to our standard!

SAM. HOUSTON,
*Commander-in-Chief of the Army.*

By order:

G. W. POE, *Acting Adjutant General.*

*No. 7.—Names of the Persons who fell at the Alamo.*

### COLONELS.

W. B. Travis, Commandant; James Bowie; David Crocket, of Tennessee.

### CAPTAINS.

— Forsyth, of the regular army; Harrison, of Tennessee; Wm. Blazeby, New Orleans Grays; — Baker, Mississippi Volunteers; — Evans; — Carey, militia of Texas; S. C. Blair, volunteer militia.

### LIEUTENANTS.

John Jones, New Orleans Grays; J. G. Baugh, New Orleans; Robert Evans, mast. ord., Ireland; — Williamson, serg't major: Dr. Michison; Dr. Pollard, surgeon; Dr. Thompson, Tennessee; Chas. Despalier; Eliel Melton, quarter-master; — Anderson, ass't qr. mast.: — Burnell, do. do.

### PRIVATES.

— Nelson; — Nelson, (clerk of Austin, mer.); William Smith, Nacogdoches; Lewis Johnson, Trinity; E. P. Mitchell, Georgia; F. Desanque, Philadelphia; John —, (clerk in Desanque's store;) — Thurston; — Moore; Christopher Parker, Natchez; — Heiskill; — Rose, Nacogdoches; — Blair, do.; David Wilson, do.; John M. Hays, Tennessee; — Stuart; — Simpson; W. D. Sutherland, Navidad, Texas; Dr. Howell, New Orleans; — Butler, do.; Charles Smith; — McGregor, Scotland; — Rusk; — Hawkins, Ireland; — Holloway; — Browne; — Smith; — Browne, Philadelphia; — Kedeson; Wm. Wells, Tennessee; Wm. Cummings, Pennsylvania; — Voluntine, do.; — Cockran; R. W. Valentine; S. Holloway; Isaac White; — Day; Robt. Musselman, New Orleans; Robt. Crossman, do.; Richard Starr, England; J. G. Ganett, New Orleans; James Dinkin, England; Robert B. Moore, New Orleans; William Linn, Boston; — Hutchinson; William Johnson, Philadelphia; — Nelson, Charleston, S. C.; George Tumlinson; Wm. Deardorf; Daniel Bourne, England; — Ingram, do.; — Lewis, Wales; Chas. Zanco, Denmark; Jas. Ewing; Robert Cunningham; — Burns, Ireland; George Neggin; Maj. G. B. Jamieson; Col. J. B. Bonham, Alabama; Capt. White; — Robinson, Scotland; — Sewell, shoemaker; — Harris, of Kentucky; — Devault, plasterer, Missouri; Jonathan Lindley, Illinois; Tapley Holland; — Dewell, blacksmith, New York; James Kinney; — Cane; — Warner; John Garvin, Missouri; — Wornel; — Robbins, Kentucky; John Flanders; Isaac Ryan, Opelousas; — Jackson, Ireland; Capt. A. Dickinson, Gonzales; Geo. C. Kimball, do.; James George, do.; Dolphin Floyd, do.; Thomas Jackson, do.; Jacob Durst, do.; George W. Cottle, do.;

Andrew Kent, do.; Thomas R. Miller, do.; Isaac Baker, do.; Wm. King, do.; Jesse McCoy, do.; Claiborn Wright, do.; William Fishback, do.; — Millsap, do.; Galby Fugua, do.; John Davis, do.; Albert Martin, do.

### No. 8.

HEAD QUARTERS OF THE ARMY,
San Jacinto, April 25, 1836.

*To His Excellency* D. G. BURNET,
*President of the Republic of Texas :*

SIR—I regret extremely that my situation since the battle of the 21st, has been such as to prevent my rendering you my official report of the same, previous to this time.

I have the honor to inform you that on the evening of the 18th inst., after a forced march of 55 miles, which was effected in two and a half days, the army arrived opposite Harrisburgh ; that eveing a courier of the enemy was taken, from which I learned that Gen. Santa Anna, with one division of his troops, had marched in the direction of Lynch's ferry, on the San Jacinto, burning Harrisburgh as he passed down. The army was ordered to be in readiness to march early the next morning. The main body effected a crossing over Buffalo Bayou, below Harrisburgh, on the morning of the 19th, having left the baggage, the sick, and a sufficient camp guard in the rear. We continued the march throughout the night, and without refreshment. At daylight we resumed the line of march, and in a short distance our scouts encountered those of the enemy, and we received information that Gen. Santa Anna was at New Washington, and would that day take up the line of march for Anahuac, crossing at Lynch's. The Texan army halted within half a mile of the ferry, in some timber, and were engaged in slaughtering beeves, when the army of Santa Anna was seen approaching in battle array, having encamped at Clopper's Point, 8 miles below. Disposition was immediately made of our forces, and preparation for his reception. He took a position, with his infantry and artillery in the centre, occupying an island of timber, his cavalry covering the left flank. The artillery then opened on our encampment, consisting of one double fortified medium brass 12-pounder.

The infantry, in columns, advanced with the design of attacking our lines, but were repulsed by a discharge of grape and canister from our artillery, consisting of two six-pounders. The enemy had occupied a piece of timber within rifle shot of the left wing of our army, from which an occasional interchange of small arms took place between the troops, until the enemy withdrew to a position on the bank of the San Jacinto, about three quarters of a mile from our encampment, and commenced a fortification. A short time before sun-set, our mounted men, about 85 in number, under the special command of Col. Sherman, marched out for the purpose of reconnoitering the enemy. Whilst advancing, they received a volley from the left of the enemy's infantry, and after a sharp rencontre with their cavalry, in which ours acted well, and performed some feats of daring chivalry, they retired in good order, having had two men severely wounded, and several horses killed. In the mean time the infantry, under the command of Lieut. Col. Millard, and Col. Bush's regiment, with the artillery, had marched out for the purpose of covering the retreat, if necessary. All those fell back in good order to our encampment about sun-set, and remained without any ostensible action until the 21st at half past 3 o'clock, taking the first refreshment which they had enjoyed for two days. The enemy, in the mean time, extended the right flank of their infantry so as to occupy the extreme point of a skirt of timber on the bank of the San Jacinto, and screened their left by a fortification about five feet high, constructed of packs and baggage, leaving an opening in the centre of the breastwork, in which their artillery was placed—the cavalry upon the left wing.

About 9 o'clock on the morning of the 21st, the enemy were reinforced by 500 choice troops, under the command of Gen. Cos, increasing their effective force to upwards of 1500 men, while our aggregate force for the field numbered 783. At half past 3 o'clock in the morning, I ordered the officers of the Texan army to parade their respective commands, having in the mean time ordered the bridges on the only road communicating with the Brazos, distant 8 miles from our encampment, to be destroyed, thus cutting off all possibility of escape. Our troops paraded with alacrity and spirit, and were anxious for the contest. Their conscious disparity in numbers only seemed to increase their enthusiasm and confidence, and heightened their anxiety for the contest. Our situation afforded me the opportunity of making the arrangements preparatory to the attack, without exposing our designs to the enemy. The 1st regiment, commanded by Col. Burleson, was assigned to the centre; the 2d regiment, under the command of Col. Sherman, formed the left wing of the army; the artillery, under the special command of Col. G. W. Herkley, Inspector General, was placed on the right of the 1st regiment; and four companies of infantry, under the command of Lieut. Col. Millard, sustained the artillery upon the right. Our cavalry, 61 in number, commanded by Col. Mirabeau B. Lamar, (whose gallant and daring conduct, on the previous day, had attracted the admiration of his comrades, and called him to that station,) placed on our extreme right, completed our line. Our cavalry was first despatched to the front of the enemy's left, for the purpose of attracting their notice, whilst an extensive island of timber afforded us an opportunity of concentrating our forces, and deploying from that point, agreeably to the previous design of the troops. Every evolution was performed with alacrity; the whole advancing rapidly in line, and through an open prairie, without any protection whatever for our men. The artillery advanced and took station within 200 yards of the enemy's breastwork, and commenced an effective fire with grape and canister.

Col. Sherman, with his regiment, having commenced the action upon our left wing, the whole line, at the centre and on the right, advancing in double quick time, rung the war cry " Remember the Alamo," received the enemy's fire, and advanced within point-blank shot before a piece was discharged from our lines. Our line advanced without a halt, until they were in possession of the woodland and the enemy's breastwork. The right wing of Burleson's, and the left of Millard's, taking possession of the breastwork ; and our artillery having gallantly charged up within 70 yards of the enemy's cannon, when it was taken by our troops. The conflict lasted about 18 minutes from the time of the close of the action until we were in possession of the enemy's encampment, taking one piece of cannon, (loaded,) four stand of colors, all their camp equipage, stores, and baggage. Our cavalry had charged and routed that of the enemy upon the right, and given pursuit to the fugitives, which did not cease until they arrived at the bridge which I mentioned before. Capt. Karnes, always among the foremost in danger, commanded the pursuers. The conflict in the breastwork lasted but a few moments ; many of the troops encountered hand to hand, and not having the advantage of bayonets on our side, our riflemen used their pieces as war clubs, breaking many of them off at the breech. The rout commenced at half past 4, and the pursuit by the main army continued until twilight. A guard was then left in charge of the enemy's encampment, and our army returned with their killed and wounded. In the battle our loss was 2 killed and 23 wounded, six of whom mortally. The enemy's loss was 630 killed, among which was 1 general officer, 4 colonels, 2 lieut. colonels, 7 captains, 12 lieutenants ; wounded 280, of which were 3 colonels, 3 lieut. colonels, 2 second lieut. colonels, 7 captains, 1 cadet. Prisoners 730—President Santa Anna, Gen. Cos, 4 colonels, aids to Gen. Santa Anna, 6 lieut. colonels, the private secretary of Gen. Santa Anna, and the colonel of the Guerrero Battalion, are included in the number. Gen. Santa Anna was not taken until the 22d, and Gen. Cos on·yesterday, very few having escaped. About 600 muskets, 300 sabres, and 200 pistols, have been collected since the action; several hundred mules and horses were taken, and near twelve thousand dollars in specie. For several days previous to the action, our troops were engaged in forced marches, exposed to excessive rains, and the additional inconvenience of extremely bad roads, ill supplied with rations and clothing; yet, amid every difficulty, they bore up with cheerfulness and fortitude, and performed their marches with speed and alacrity—there was no murmuring.

Previous to and during the action, my Staff evinced every disposition to be useful, and were actively engaged in their duties. In the conflict, I am assured that they demeaned themselves in such manner as proved them worthy members of the army of San Jacinto. Col. T. J. Rusk, Secretary of War, was on the field; for weeks his services had been highly beneficial to the army; in battle he was on the left wing, where Col. Sherman's command first encountered and drove the enemy; he bore himself gallantly, and continued his efforts and activity, remaining with the pursuers until resistance ceased.     *     *     *     *     *     *

For the Commanding General to attempt discrimination as to the conduct of those who commanded in the action, or those who were commanded, would be impossible : our success in the action is conclusive proof of their daring intrepidity and courage. Every officer and man proved himself worthy of the cause in which he battled, while the triumph received a lustre, from the humanity which characterised their conduct after victory, and richly entitles them to the admiration and gratitude of their General. Nor should we withhold the tribute of our grateful thanks from that Being who rules the destinies of nations, and has, in the time of the greatest need, enabled us to arrest a powerful invader whilst devastating our country.

I have the honor to be, with high consideration,

Your obedient servant,

SAMUEL HOUSTON,

*Commander-in-Chief.*

# The Far Western Frontier

An Arno Press Collection

[Angel, Myron, editor]. **History of Nevada.** 1881.

Barnes, Demas. **From the Atlantic to the Pacific, Overland.** 1866.

Beadle, J[ohn] H[anson]. **The Undeveloped West; Or, Five Years in the Territories.** [1873].

Bidwell, John. **Echoes of the Past:** An Account of the First Emigrant Train to California. [1914].

Bowles, Samuel. **Our New West.** 1869.

Browne, J[ohn] Ross. **Adventures in the Apache Country.** 1871.

Browne, J[ohn] Ross. **Report of the Debates in the Convention of California, on the Formation of the State Constitution.** 1850.

Byers, W[illiam] N. and J[ohn] H. Kellom. **Hand Book to the Gold Fields of Nebraska and Kansas.** 1859.

Carvalho, S[olomon] N. **Incidents of Travel and Adventure in the Far West; with Col. Fremont's Last Expedition Across the Rocky Mountains.** 1857.

Clayton, William. **William Clayton's Journal.** 1921.

Cooke, P[hilip] St. G[eorge]. **Scenes and Adventures in the Army.** 1857.

Cornwallis, Kinahan. **The New El Dorado; Or, British Columbia.** 1858.

Davis, W[illiam] W. H. **El Gringo; Or, New Mexico and Her People.** 1857.

De Quille, Dan. (William Wright). **A History of the Comstock Silver Lode & Mines.** 1889.

Delano, A[lonzo]. **Life on the Plains and Among the Diggings;** Being Scenes and Adventures of an Overland Journey to California. 1854.

Ferguson, Charles D. **The Experiences of a Forty-niner in California.** (Originally published as *The Experiences of a Forty-niner During Thirty-four Years' Residence in California and Australia*). 1888.

Forbes, Alexander. **California:** A History of Upper and Lower California. 1839.

Fossett, Frank. **Colorado:** Its Gold and Silver Mines, Farms and Stock Ranges, and Health and Pleasure Resorts. 1879.

**The Gold Mines of California:** Two Guidebooks. 1973.

Gray, W[illiam] H[enry]. **A History of Oregon, 1792–1849.** 1870.

Green, Thomas J. **Journal of the Texian Expedition Against Mier.** 1845.

Henry, W[illiam] S[eaton]. **Campaign Sketches of the War with Mexico.** 1847.

[Hildreth, James]. **Dragoon Campaigns to the Rocky Mountains.** 1836.

Hines, Gustavus. **Oregon:** Its History, Condition and Prospects. 1851.

Holley, Mary Austin. **Texas:** Observations, Historical, Geographical and Descriptive. 1833.

Hollister, Ovando J[ames]. **The Mines of Colorado.** 1867.

Hughes, John T. **Doniphan's Expedition.** 1847.

Johnston, W[illiam] G. **Experiences of a Forty-niner.** 1892.

Jones, Anson. **Memoranda and Official Correspondence Relating to the Republic of Texas, Its History and Annexation.** 1859.

Kelly, William. **An Excursion to California Over the Prairie, Rocky Mountains, and Great Sierra Nevada.** 1851. 2 Volumes in 1.

Lee, D[aniel] and J[oseph] H. Frost. **Ten Years in Oregon.** 1844.

Macfie, Matthew. **Vancouver Island and British Columbia.** 1865.

Marsh, James B. **Four Years in the Rockies; Or, the Adventures of Isaac P. Rose.** 1884.

Mowry, Sylvester. **Arizona and Sonora:** The Geography, History, and Resources of the Silver Region of North America. 1864.

Mullan, John. **Miners and Travelers' Guide to Oregon, Washington, Idaho, Montana, Wyoming, and Colorado.** 1865.

Newell, C[hester]. **History of the Revolution in Texas.** 1838.

Parker, A[mos] A[ndrew]. **Trip to the West and Texas.** 1835.

Pattie, James O[hio]. **The Personal Narrative of James O. Pattie, of Kentucky.** 1831.

Rae, W[illiam] F[raser]. **Westward by Rail:** The New Route to the East. 1871.

Ryan, William Redmond. **Personal Adventures in Upper and Lower California, in 1848–9.** 1850/1851. 2 Volumes in 1.

Shaw, William. **Golden Dreams and Waking Realities:** Being the Adventures of a Gold-Seeker in California and the Pacific Islands. 1851.

Stuart, Granville. **Montana As It Is:** Being a General Description of its Resources. 1865.

**Texas in 1840, Or the Emigrant's Guide to the New Republic.** 1840.

Thornton, J. Quinn. **Oregon and California in 1848.** 1849. 2 Volumes in 1.

Upham, Samuel C. **Notes of a Voyage to California via Cape Horn, Together with Scenes in El Dorado, in the Years 1849–'50.** 1878.

Woods, Daniel B. **Sixteen Months at the Gold Diggings.** 1851.

Young, F[rank] G., editor. **The Correspondence and Journals of Captain Nathaniel J. Wyeth, 1831–6.** 1899.

DAVID GLENN HUNT
MEMORIAL LIBRARY
GALVESTON COLLEGE